The Friends of Durruti Group: 1937–1939

Agustin Guillamón

Translated by
Paul Sharkey

AK PRESS

The Friends of Durruti Group 1937–1939
ISBN 1-873176-54-6

Library of Congress Cataloging-in-Publication Data
A catalog record for this title is available from the Library of Congress.

British Library Cataloguing-in-Publication Data
A catalogue record for this title is available from the British Library.

The Friends of Durruti Group 1937–1939 was published orginally in Spanish in Cuaderno Número 3 of *Balance*, serie de estudios e investigaciones [Balance, Apartado 22010, Barcelona]

This English-language edition published by:

AK Press	AK Press
P.O. Box 12766	P.O. Box 40682
Edinburgh, Scotland	San Francisco, CA
EH8 9YE	94140-0682

An enormous thank you is offered to comrade Frederico Arcos for allowing AK Press access to his copies of *El Amigo del Pueblo* to illustrate this book.

Design and layout work donated by Freddie Baer.

Contents

EL AMIGO DEL PUEBLO

PORTAVOZ DE LOS AMIGOS DE DURRUTI

Año I - Núm 1 Redacción y Administración: Rambla de las Flores, 1, 1.º - Teléfono 15,721 20 céntimos

Unos colores matizan la epopeya ibérica. - Una bandera encarnó el despertar de las jornadas de julio.

Envuelta en los pliegues de la enseña rojinegra surgió nuestro proletariado a la superficie hispánica con ansias de emancipación absoluta.

Un hombre floreció en aquellos sublimes jornadas. Buenaventura Durruti tomó raigambre humana en el corazón de las multitudes. Luchó por los trabajadores. Murió por ellos. Su pasado inmortal está ceñido a esta bandera roji-negra que flameó gallardamente en los albores de julio majestuoso. De su ataud la tomamos al descargarlo de nuestros hombros. Con ella en alto, caeremos o venceremos. No hay términos medios: o vencer, o caer.

¿No somos provocadores? ¿Somos los mismos de siempre?
Durruti es nuestro guía! Su bandera es la nuestra!

¡Nadie nos la arrebatará! Es nuestra!
Viva la F. A. I.! Viva la C. N. T.!

Preface to the English-language Edition of *The Friends of Durruti Group 1937–1939*

Agustin Guillamón's monograph on the Friends of Durruti Group affords readers of English the most comprehensive and thorough exploration and account of the history and ideas of that group. Few groups if any have suffered from such widespread misunderstanding, exaggeration and interested misrepresentation. Guillamón has brought new evidence to light and disposes effectively of some of the most enduring misrepresentations.

Liberals, Stalinists, marxists and libertarians have vied with one another in their condemnation and misrepresentation of the group and its message. Italian Stalinists accounted association with the group grounds enough upon which to execute political opponents. On May 29, 1937, the Italian Communist Party paper *Il Grido del Popolo* carried an item which referred to Camillo Berneri as "one of the leaders of the 'Friends of Durruti' Group, which (...) provoked the bloody insurrection against the Popular Front Government in Catalonia [and] was given his just desserts during that revolt at the hands of the Democratic Revolution, whose legitimate right of self-defense no antifascist can deny." There is no evidence at all to connect Berneri with the Friends of Durruti. On behalf of the "Errico Malatesta" group, Domenico Ludovici, an Italian anarchist, retorted that "The unfortunate comrade Berneri was not a member of the 'Friends of Durruti' Group, not that there would be anything wrong in that and it would never excuse the cowardly murder of which he was the victim. No doubt the democratic 'journalist' from *Il Grido del Popolo* must be a co-religionist of the perpetrators of the barbarous act hence the concern to represent the 'Friends of Durruti' as the provocateurs of the bloodshed, which everybody, the whole world, save *Il Grido del Popolo*, knows were of 'democratic' derivation."[1] Curious that the Italian anarchists of the Ascaso Column, whose scrupulous commitment to principle over pragmatism frequently set them at odds with their Spanish colleagues, seem to have found little if anything to criticize in the performance of the Friends of Durruti. Even with the benefit of ten years of hindsight, Ernesto Bonomini could speak approvingly of the group.[2]

As to the allegation that the Friends of Durruti had instigated the fighting in Barcelona in May, they rebutted that when it came from *Las Noticias*. "They must think us real idiots, because, had the groups they named [the Friends of Durruti and the Libertarian Youth] been the instigators of the revolt, no way would we have surrendered the streets."[3]

If the Friends of Durruti certainly did not instigate the events of May 1937, they equally certainly were among the few with a ready response to them. They had been alive to the encroachments of the revived Catalan State and bourgeoisie for quite some time and had been yearning for a return to the uncomplicated radical confrontations that had brought such promise with the victory over the fascists in July 1936.[4] Such a feeling was a rather diffuse presence in many sectors of the libertarian movement in Catalonia. The dalliance of the organizations' higher committees with politicians and their pursuit of a unified and disciplined policy as an aid to them in their dealings with the latter had led to certain unwelcome changes in the everyday practices of those organizations. By January 1937 *Ideas* was issuing reminders of the proprieties of trade union federalism with the capitalized warning: **"The so-called higher committees ought to be bound by the accords of the trade union organization. The unions dispose and the committees see to it that the dispositions are implemented. That is what federalism is, whatever else is done is dictatorship and that cannot be tolerated for one minute more."**[5] That same month the Libertarian Youth paper *Ruta* was pointedly reminding its readers that "All we can expect of self-sufficing minorities seeking to set themselves up as infallible guides is dictatorship and oppression."[6]

There seem to have been three major preoccupations among those uneasy with the stagnation and ebbing of the revolution: 1. the attempt to relegate the revolution to second place behind the war effort; 2. the erosion of accountability of the higher committees; 3. the suspicion that some compromise resolution brokered by outside powers was being hatched.[7] Many reckoned that their very own leaders had been seduced and corrupted by association with politicians.

The Friends of Durruti shared and addressed all of these concerns. Alone among all the dissidents in the libertarian camp, they sought to devise a coherent set of alternatives. But the enforcement of discipline and the strength of sentimental attachment to organizations hobbled their efforts and reduced their audience. The mixture of discipline and sentiment is clearly seen in the letter which two members of the Friends of Durruti published in the pages of *Solidaridad Obrera* on May 29, 1937. Following a threat by the regional committees of the CNT and FAI and by the CNT's Local Federation in Barcelona to expel all members of the Friends who failed to publicly disassociate themselves from the Group, Joaquin Aubi and Rosa Muñoz resigned from it, albeit specifying that "I continue to regard the comrades belonging to the 'Friends of Durruti' as comrades: but I say again what I have always said at plenums in Barcelona: 'The CNT has been my womb and the CNT will be my tomb.'"

That dictum in fact could serve as an epitaph for the Friends of Durruti as a whole. It does not appear that the committees' decision to proceed with expulsions was ever activated, and that in itself seems to confirm the degree of rank and file support for the Friends, as does the CNT national plenum of regionals' endorsement of Catalonia's intention to "expel from the Organization the *leading lights* of the 'Friends of Durruti' Group and to take whatever steps are necessary to ensure that no split ensues as a consequence of this."[8]

Again the Friends had to remind their "superiors" of the norms of the organization. No one ever joined the CNT, the Confederation. All CNT members belonged to local unions and federations and sovereignty resided in these. **"We can only be expelled from the confederal organization by the assemblies of the unions. Local and comarcal plenums are not empowered to expel any comrade. We invite the committees to raise the matter of the 'Friends of Durruti' in the assemblies, which is where the organization's sovereignty resides."**[9]

A similar concern with constitutional procedure can be seen in the Friends' reaction to the news that the arch-Treintista Angel Pestaña, leader of the Syndicalist Party, had been readmitted into the CNT fold. "We cannot understand how Pestaña had been admitted without having been required to wind up his Syndicalist Party, a precondition stipulated on other occasions when there was talk of his possibly rejoining."[10]

Preoccupied as it was with preserving the CNT-FAI's clout within the Republican coalition, the leadership of that conglomerate was ever alert to infiltration and to abuse of its initials. And prompt to see threats of both in the Friends. There were dark hints of "marxism", due to certain common ground in the declarations of the minuscule Bolshevik-Leninist contingent and of the Friends, as well as the Friends' non-sectarian acknowledgment of how the POUM had acquitted itself during the street-fighting in May. Here again, misrepresentation has been rife. Balius was moved to challenge his detractors to substantiate the charges of "marxist" leveled or whispered against him.[11] Guillamón deals definitively with the allegations of POUM and Trotskyist connections, laying those allegations to rest. Less easily disposed of is the mythology surrounding what the Friends themselves recognized was a "slight innovation," the Revolutionary Junta.

The first thing that needs to be said is that Junta in Spanish does not have the same pejorative connotation as it does in English. Each CNT union was run by a Junta. In Mexico, the Mexican Liberal Party of the brothers Magón was run by a Junta. So the word itself carries no suggestion of authoritarianism.

The next point to be made plain is that the Friends were agitating for a Junta, not reporting the formation of one. Had they actually formed one and admitted the POUM into it alongside themselves, then the charges of "anarcho-Bolshevism" sometimes leveled against them, might stand up on the basis of that substitutionism. But no Junta was ever formed, in spite of what José Peirats among others claims.[12]

One of the most invidious representations, or *mis*representations regarding the Friends has been the decision by César M. Lorenzo to incorporate into the footnotes of his book *Los anarquistas españoles y el poder* (Paris, 1972) of a reference to a *Manifiesto de Unión Communista* purporting to speak for the 'Friends of Durruti', the POUM and certain elements of the Libertarian Youth. On the face of it, this clinches the case for the Friends' having associated, indeed amalgamated themselves with marxist elements in a self-appointed vanguard union. But it is nothing of the sort. Lorenzo states that the manifesto was "distributed at the beginning of the month of June," without specifying where.[13] In fact, the text he cites comes from a leaflet distributed *in Paris* at the Velodrome d'Hiver on June 16, 1937 by militants of the tiny French Union Communiste organization by way of a retort to Garcia Oliver and Federica Montseny, to contrast their official CNT-FAI line with the revolutionism displayed by the three named groups in May 1937. Whether Lorenzo's failure to make this clear is due to an oversight or to its serving his purposes in representing the Friends as an anarcho-Bolshevik formation is unclear, but the misrepresentation has been taken up uncritically by others and contributed to the shadow of ignorance hanging over the group and its ideas.[14]

Union Communiste stole a march on anarchist sympathizers with the Friends (such as Andre Prudhommeaux) by publishing translations of articles from *El Amigo del Pueblo* in its own paper, *L'Internationale* in December 1937. Union Communiste somewhat overstates the case, however, when it added the comment that: "What the Friends of Durruti cannot say within the narrow confines of an editorial in a clandestine publication is that this revolutionary theory is the handiwork of a vanguard. The necessity of revolutionary theory implies the necessity of an organized vanguard, thrown up by the struggle, which debates and devises the elements of the revolution's program. The necessity, therefore, of a "party", or, since this word party has been overused to mean treacherous organizations, of a banding together of the most clear-sighted, most active, most committed workers." And their prediction that "... the Friends of Durruti will assuredly continue this trend which brought them into association with the left-wing elements of the POUM and which may lead them to the constitution of the revolutionary party that the Spanish proletariat lacked in the battles of recent years", was well wide of the mark, as Guillamón makes plain.[15]

That there were certain questions raised but not quite clarified in the pages of *El Amigo del Pueblo* and in the Group's fuller manifesto *Towards of Fresh Revolution* cannot be denied. The Friends were making an honest effort to articulate in an anarchist idiom what they thought might provide a way out of the impasse of their much-abused generosity towards other antifascists and a second wind to the revolution which had been so denatured by collaboration under the umbrella of antifascism. One recurrent phrase is their claim that revolutionaries had to **quemar una etapa** (step things up a notch). They sought to re-found antifascism by asserting the hegemony of the working class libertarian element, ensuring that due recompense was received for effort expended. They sought to reinvigorate the trade unions which had become, if not moribund, then at least less vibrant, by reclaiming their autonomy and reasserting the protagonism lost to collaboration.[16]

More recently, a rather absurd reading of the facts surrounding the Friends of Durruti and the character of Jaime Balius has emerged from the pens of a duo of Spanish academic historians, Enric Ucelay da Cal and Susana Tavera. Starting from the laudable intention of tracing the group dynamics within libertarian circles in Catalonia and with special reference to the ensconcement of Jacinto Toryho as editor of *Solidaridad Obrera* and as the spokesman for the "official line" of the CNT-FAI in Catalonia, the authors concoct a Machiavellian tale of Balius's frustrated journalistic ambition festering into cynical exploitation of the misgivings and resentments of dissenting libertarians. Guillamón rightly dismisses the article in question as "nonsense," "outrageous" and "derogatory" and it would be a pity if the authors' academic distinction were to breathe life into what is unquestionably a very shabby and shoddy piece of historical research, all the more aggravating for the pair's self-congratulation. Their concoction offers the reader a description of the launching of the Friends of Durruti in March 1937 as "an attempt to inject significant political content into personal frustration, singling out as the enemy the counter-revolution and the Stalinists and, to a lesser extent, those responsible for his [Balius's] displacement within the CNT."[17]

Agustin Guillamón is to be congratulated for having undertaken his research in a spirit of scientific inquiry. He deals comprehensively with the usual fictions and offers us a scrupulously accurate account of the ideas and objectives of what remains the most fascinating and most articulate of the dissenting groups within the greater family of Spanish libertarianism in the crucial year of 1937.

Notes to the Preface

1. Writing in *Ideas* (Bajo Llobregat) No 24, June 17, 1937, p. 4.
2. Ernesto Bonomini wrote an eyewitness account of the May events in Barcelona for *Volonta* No 11, May 1, 1947.
3. *El Amigo del Pueblo* No 4, June 22, 1937, p. 3, "El asalto a la Telefónica".
4. Spanish anarchism was more comfortable with radical contrasts than with the blurred edges created by, say, the antifascist umbrella, or, earlier, republican ralliement. "We Spanish anarcho-syndicalists were faithful to the dialectical principle to the very end. Liberal or reformist government we made an especial target of our spleen, out of a secret feeling of competition. We would rather unemployment lines than unemployment benefit. Given a choice between enslavement to bosses and cooperativism, we preferred the former. And emphatically rejected the latter." — José Peirats *Examen criticoconstructivo del Movimiento Libertario Español* (Editores Mexicanos Unidos, Mexico DF, 1967) p. 42.
5. *Ideas* No 4, January 21, 1937, p. 4.
6. *Ruta* (Barcelona) No 13, January 7, 1937, p. 6, "Centralismo."
7. Boldly displayed on the front page of *El Amigo del Pueblo* No 2, May 26, 1937, was this item: "**We are against any armistice**. The blood shed by Spanish workers is an impregnable bulwark upon which the intrigues sponsored by home-grown politicians and capitalist diplomats around the world will founder. Victory or death. There is no other solution." Similar defiance of suspected intrigues designed to bring about a diplomatic resolution of the war and taking things out of the hands of Spanish workers featured in *Ideas*, *Ruta* and other papers also.
8. José Peirats *La CNT en la revolución española* (Ed. Madre Tierra, Madrid, 1988, Vol. 11, p. 220) citing a CNT National Committee resume of the accords reached at a national plenum of regionals meeting on May 23, 1937.
9. *El Amigo del Pueblo* No 2, 26 May 1937, p. 3. The Friends pointedly added: **"Whenever, in contravention of every confederal precept, someone goes over the heads of assemblies and militants and sets himself up as a general,**

making mistake after mistake, he has no option, assuming he has any shred of dignity left, but to set down. Garcia Oliver fits that bill!"

10. *El Amigo del Pueblo* No 8, September 21, 1937, p. 2. "The admission of Pestana sets the seal upon the bourgeois democratic mentality in a broad swathe of confederal circles. Watch out, comrades."

11. *El Amigo del Pueblo* No 4, June 22, 1937, p. 3, "**En defensa propia:** Necesito una aclaración." "I am aghast at countless instances of my being labeled a marxist, because I am 100 percent a revolutionary." This comment suggests that Balius regarded marxists as being something short of 100 percent revolutionaries, although the Friends were generous enough to recognize that the POUM had acquitted itself well in the street-fighting in Barcelona in May 1937. This rejection of marxism would have applied not to the marxian analysis of capitalist economics, but to the marxist recipe for changing society, not to the *descriptive* but to the *prescriptive* element.

12. José Peirats *La CNT en la revolución española* Vol 11, p. 147. Peirats reproduces a text which opens "A Revolutionary Junta **has been formed** [emphasis added] in Barcelona." César M. Lorenzo reproduces this text given by Peirats. But the Peirats text is not a quotation but a mistaken paraphrase.

13. César M. Lorenzo *Los anarquistas espanoles y el poder* (Ruedo Iberico, Paris, 1972) p. 219, n. 32.

14. The full text of the leaflet from which Lorenzo quotes can be found in Henri Chaze *Chronique de la revolution espagnole: Union Communiste (1933–1939)* (Paris, Cahiers Spartacus, 1979) pp. 114-115. Juan Gómez Casas *Anarchist Organization: The History of the FAI* (Black Rose Books, Montreal-Buffalo, 1986, p. 210) uncritically reproduces Lorenzo's curious footnote as if it were a Friends of Durruti text.

15. Henri Chaze, op. cit. p. 82 (from *L'Internationale* No 33, December 18, 1937.

16. Exasperation with their republican "allies" was widespread by the summer of 1937 and before. There were even embarrassed arguments about the ingenuousness of anarchists. "Let us make very plain the principle that we owe no loyalty to him who is disloyal with us: that we owe no respect to him who secretly betrays us, that we have no duty of tolerance to anyone disposed to coerce us just as soon as he is strong enough to do so and get away with it, that principle cannot oblige us to respect the freedom of him whose principle is to take away our freedom" (Beobachter, in *Ideas* No 29, August 6, 1937).

17. Susana Tavera and Enric Ucelay Da Cal "Grupos de afinidad, disciplina bélica y periodismo libertario 1936–1938" in *Historia Contemporanea*, 9, (Servicio Ed. Universidad del Pais Vasco, 1993) pp. 184.

EL AMIGO DEL PUEBLO

PORTAVOZ DE LOS AMIGOS DE DURRUTI

Año I – Núm. 2 – 20 Cts. – Redacción y Administración: Rambla de las Flores, 1, 1.º – Teléfono 15,721 – Miércoles, 30 Mayo de 1937

Nuestro camarada Francisco Ascaso cayó al pie de Atarazanas. La sangre derramada en aquellas jornadas de Julio, persiste todavía en nuestro recuerdo.

El trato indigno que nos dan en censura, nos obliga a burlarla. Es una vergüenza y una ignominia la desfachatez de tacharnos los comentarios más insignificantes. No podemos ni queremos tolerarlo.

¡Siervos, no!

Propósitos de mediación

El fracaso de la ofensiva fascista en Euzkadi y la heroica resistencia de los camaradas de la Castilla [illegible], ha desbaratado todos los planes del fascio internacional en la península ibérica.

Se habla con cierta insistencia en los círculos del mundillo diplomático, de una posible retirada de las fuerzas alemanas e italianas del suelo español.

Al mismo tiempo que estos rumores han sido [illegible], se han multiplicado las conversaciones diplomáticas entre los altos dignatarios de las principales potencias que luchan por la supremacía en el continente europeo.

Los dirigentes de la política francesa e inglesa [illegible] a la guerra que sostienen los trabajadores españoles. Se busca, con [illegible], la fórmula que permita dejar las cosas de España de una manera tal que se pueda restablecer los privilegios de las castas contra las cuales se levantó el proletariado ibérico en las memorables jornadas de julio.

Nos oponemos a todo armisticio

La sangre derramada por los trabajadores españoles, es un valladar infranqueable en el que se estrellarán los manejos que patrocinan los políticos indígenas y la diplomacia capitalista del mundo entero.

Vencer o morir. No cabe otra solución.

Las potencias fascistas quieren salir airosas de la aventura en que se embarcaron. Alemania, que ha llevado el pleito iniciado en el salón de los espejos de Versalles a territorio ibérico, [illegible]. Y el Duce necesita que se le [illegible] que, al propio tiempo, [illegible] quebrado.

Para nuestra lucha tiene [illegible]. Nuestra revolución amenaza todos los imperialismos. El heroísmo de nuestros trabajadores [illegible] del mundo. Las colonias [illegible] por los Estados capitalistas y los trabajadores del mundo entero, tienen puesta su vista en nuestra epopeya. [illegible] un peligro evidente de que [illegible].

Por estas razones los Estados fascistas, las potencias democráticas, tienen un interés especial en ahogar la guerra que sostenemos, que es la propia revolución armada. Nosotros no cejaremos en la lucha.

1. Introduction and Chronology

The Friends of Durruti were an anarchist affinity group founded in March 1937. Its members were militians with the Durruti Column opposed to militarization and/or anarchists critical of the CNT's entry into the Republican government and the Generalidad government.

The historical and political importance of the Friends of Durruti Group lies in **its attempt**, emanating from within the ranks of the libertarian movement itself (in 1937) **to constitute a revolutionary vanguard** that would put paid to departures from revolutionary principles and to collaboration with the capitalist State: leaving the CNT to defend and press home the "gains" of July 1936, instead of surrendering them little by little to the bourgeoisie.

This edition of *Balance* examines the process whereby the Friends of Durruti emerged, their ideological characteristics and the evolution of their political thinking, their dealings with the Trotskyists, and the reasons behind the failure of their fight to recover anarcho-syndicalism's doctrinal purity and salvage the Spanish revolution of 1936.

There follows a chronology which, though selective rather than exhaustive, contains heretofore unpublished information. This chronology is intended to afford familiarity with the essential historical events, so that the arguments spelled out in this study may be more readily and strictly comprehensible.

Chronology

July 17-21, 1936: Servicemen and fascists rebel against the government of the Republic. Where the workers offer armed resistance, the rebels fail, securing victory only where there are attempts at conciliation or no armed confrontation. Civil war erupts.

July 21, 1936: Establishment in Catalonia of the Central Anti-Fascist Militias Committee (CAMC). No workers' organization takes power.

August 19-25, 1936: Trial of the Sixteen in Moscow. Zinoviev, Kamenev and Smirnov executed. Radek placed under arrest.

September 26, 1936: Three anarchists — Doménech, Fábregas and Garcia Birlan — join the Generalidad government in Catalonia.

October 2, 1936: the CAMC is wound up.

October 12, 1936: A Generalidad decree dissolves the (revolutionary) Local Committees. These are shortly to be replaced by new, Popular Front-style town councils.

October 27, 1936: A Generalidad decree orders militarization of the People's Militias.

November 4, 1936: Four anarchist ministers — Garcia Oliver, Frederica Montseny, Joan Peiró and Juan López — join the Republic's government.

November 5, 1936: Durruti makes a radio broadcast from the Madrid front, in which he opposes the decree issued by the Generalidad militarizing the militias, and calls for greater commitment and sacrifice from the rearguard if the war is to be won.

November 6, 1936: The Republic's government (along with the four new anarcho-syndicalist ministers) flees Madrid for the safety of Valencia. The populace of Madrid's response is the cry of "Long live Madrid without government!"

November 7, 1936: the International Brigades intervene on the Madrid front.

November 9, 1936: Formation of the Madrid Defense Junta.

November 20, 1936: Durruti loses his life on the Madrid front.

December 6, 1936: In *Solidaridad Obrera*, Balius publishes an article entitled "Durruti's Testament" in which he states: "Durruti bluntly asserted that we anarchists require that the Revolution be totalitarian in character."

December 16, 1936: the POUM is excluded from the Generalidad government.

December 21, 1936: Stalin offers advice to Largo Caballero.

December 29, 1936: Publication of issue No. 1 of *Ideas.*

January 26, 1937: Balius appointed director of *La Noche.*

February 5-8, 1937: Plenary assembly of the confederal and anarchist militias meeting in Valencia to consider the militarization issue.

March 4, 1937: the newspaper *La Noche* carries an announcement introducing the aims, characteristics and membership conditions of the Friends of Durruti Group.

March 4, 1937: the Generalidad issues a decree winding up the Control Patrols. In *La Batalla,* Nin passes favorable and hopeful comment on an article by Balius carried in the March 2nd edition of *La Noche.*

March 11, 1937: *Ideas* calls for the dismissal of Aiguadé.

March 17, 1937: the Friends of Durruti Group is formally established. Balius is appointed vice-secretary. Ruiz and Carreño are on its steering committee.

March 21, 1937: the Iron Column meets in assembly to vote on militarization or disbandment: it agrees to militarization.

Late March–early April 1937: A flyer bearing the endorsement of the Friends of Durruti Group is issued.

April 8, 1937: In *Ideas,* Balius has an article published entitled "Let's make revolution," in which he says: "if [Companys] had a larger contingent of armed forces at his disposal, he would have the working class back in the capitalist harness."

April 14, 1937: the Friends of Durruti issue a manifesto opposing the commemoration of the anniversary of the proclamation of the Republic.

(Sunday) April 18, 1937: The Friends of Durruti hold a rally in the Poliorama Theater. Chaired by Romero, it hears contributions from Francisco Pellicer, Pablo Ruiz, Jaime Balius, Francisco Carreño and V. Pérez Combina.

April 25, 1937: the UGT leader Roldán Cortada is murdered in Molins del Llobregat.

April 27 and 28, 1937: Armed conflict between anarchists and Generalidad forces in Bellver de Cerdaña. Antonio Martin, the anarchist mayor of Puigcerdá, is shot dead.

Late April 1937: A poster from the Group is pinned up on trees and walls throughout the city of Barcelona. In it, the Friends of Durruti set out their program: "All power to the working class. All economic power to the unions. Instead of the Generalidad, the Revolutionary Junta."

(Saturday) May 1, 1937: An ordinary working day, for the Generalidad has banned commemoration of the First of May, in an effort to avert disturbances and confrontations. The Generalidad government meets in session, congratulating its Commissar for Public Order on the successes achieved. A panel is made up of Tarradellas (Prime Councilor), Rodriguez Salas (Commissar for Public Order) and Artemi Aiguadé (Councilor for Internal Security): it promptly holds a meeting behind closed doors to tackle urgent business relating to public order and security. The Bolshevik-Leninist Section issues a leaflet.

(Sunday) May 2, 1937: Friends of Durruti rally in the Goya Theater, at which the film "19 de julio" is screened to comments from Balius: there are speeches by Liberto Callejas and Francisco Carreño as well. CNT militants interrupt a telephone conversation between Companys and Azana.

(Monday) May 3, 1937: A little before 3:00 P.M. three truckloads of Guards commanded by Rodriguez Salas attempt to seize the Telephone Exchange, on the orders of Artemi Aiguadé. Armed resistance from the CNT workers on the upper floors thwarts this. Within a few hours, a host of armed bands has been formed and the first barricades erected. The mobilization resolves into two sides: one made up of the CNT and the POUM, the other of the Generalidad, the PSUC, the ERC and Estat Català. Businesses close down. The train service stops at 7:00 P.M. At that hour, in the Casa CNT-FAI in the Via Durruti, the CNI Regional Committee and the POUM Executive Committee meet. The maximum demand is that Rodriguez Salas and Artemi Aiguadé resign. Companys doggedly opposes this.

(Tuesday) May 4, 1937: Gun-battles throughout the night. Many barricades and violent clashes throughout the city. In the Sants barrio 400 Guards are stripped of their weapons. Companys asks the Valencia government for aircraft to bomb the CNT's premises and barracks.[2] The CNT-controlled artillery on Montjuich and Tibidabo is trained on the Generalidad Palace.[3] Abad de Santillán, Isgleas and Molina manage to halt in Lerida, "en route to Barcelona," the divisions despatched by the CNT's Máximo Franco (a Friends of Durruti member) and the POUM's José Rovira. At 7:00 P.M. in the Principal Palace in the Ramblas, which has been commandeered by the POUM, Jaime Balius, Pablo Ruiz, Eleuterio Roig and Martin, representing the Friends of Durruti, meet Gorkin, Nin and Andrade, representing the POUM's Executive Committee. Following an analysis of the situation, and in view of the stance adopted by the CNT, they come to an agreement to suggest an orderly armed withdrawal of combatants from the barricades. At 9:00 P.M. the Generalidad radio station issues an appeal from the leaders of the various organizations (Garcia Oliver representing the CNT) for an end to fighting. The POUM Executive Committee releases a manifesto. The Bolshevik-Leninist Section issues a handbill. On the night of May 4-5, the Friends of Durruti Group drafts and prints up a handbill.

(Wednesday) May 5, 1937: A handbill is distributed by the Friends of Durruti. Over the radio, the CNT disowns the Friends of Durruti Group. Fighting is now confined to the city center: the rest of the city being in the hands of the confederal Defense Committees. At 1:00 P.M. the UGT leader Sesé, a recently appointed Generalidad councilor perishes in gunfire emanating from the premises of the CNT's Entertainments Union. At 3:00 P.M. the Generalidad transmitter issues a fresh appeal for calm from the leaders of the various organizations (Federica Montseny for the CNT). A brother of Ascaso is killed. Berneri and Barbieri are arrested by Guards and UGT militants from the Water Union. Their corpses show up later.

(Thursday) May 6, 1937: *La Batalla* reprints the Friends of Durruti handbill. In the same edition, *La Batalla* appeals for workers to back down. *Solidaridad Obrera* disowns the Friends of Durruti handbill .

(Friday) May 7, 1937: *La Batalla* reiterates its appeal, making it conditional upon withdrawal of the security forces and retention of weapons. Transport services are restored and a degree of normality returns. Assault Guards sent by the Valencia government reach Barcelona around 9:00 P.M. Companys surrenders control of public order. The Control Patrols place themselves at the disposal of the special delegate in charge of public order sent down by the Republican government.

(Saturday) May 8, 1937: Barricades are dismantled, except for the PSUC barricades, which persist into June. The Friends of Durruti distribute a manifesto reviewing the events of May. In that manifesto there is talk of "treachery" by the CNT leadership.

(Sunday) May 9, 1937: *Solidaridad Obrera* dismisses the manifesto as demagoguery and the Group's members as provocateurs.

May 17, 1937: Negrin takes over from Largo Caballero as premier. The UGT Regional Committee for Catalonia demands that all POUM militants be expelled from its ranks and presses the CNT to mete out the same treatment to the Friends of Durruti.

May 19, 1937: Issue No. 1 of *El Amigo del Pueblo* appears.

May 22, 1937: A plenary session of the CNT's Local and Comarcal Federations hears a proposal that the Friends of Durruti be expelled. A session of the Sabadell city council agrees that councilor Bruno Lladó Roca (also the Generalidad's comarcal delegate for Economy) be stood down for having displayed a Friends of Durruti poster in his office.

May 26, 1937: Issue No. 2 of *El Amigo del Pueblo* appears, having evaded the censor. Balius is jailed a few days later as the director of a clandestine publication, following a complaint from the PSUC.

May 28, 1937: *La Batalla* is shut down as is the POUM's radio station. The Friends of Durruti's social premises in the Ramblas are shut down.

June 6, 1937: The Control Patrols are disbanded.

June 12, 1937: *El Amigo del Pueblo* No. 3.

June 16, 1937: The members of the POUM Executive Committee are rounded up. The POUM is proscribed and its militants persecuted.

June 22, 1937: *El Amigo del Pueblo* No. 4.

June 22-24, 1937: Andrés Nin is kidnapped and murdered by the Soviet secret police.

June 26, 1937: Showing solidarity with the POUM militants persecuted by the Stalinists and the Republic's police, the Bolshevik-Leninist Section calls for concerted action by the Section, the left of the POUM and the Friends of Durruti.

July 2, 1937: A handbill from the Bolshevik-Leninist Section of Spain (on behalf of the Fourth International) expresses solidarity with the POUM militants persecuted by the Stalinists.

July 20, 1937: *El Amigo del Pueblo* No. 5.

August 10, 1937: The Council of Aragon is forcibly disbanded by the government.

August 12, 1937: El *Amigo del Pueblo* No. 6.

August 31, 1937: *El Amigo del Pueblo* No. 7.

September 21, 1937: *El Amigo del Pueblo* No. 8.

October 20, 1937: *El Amigo del Pueblo* No. 9.

November 8, 1937: *El Amigo del Pueblo* No. 10.

November 20, 1937: *El Amigo del Pueblo* No. 11.

January 1938: *Towards a Fresh Revolution* pamphlet drafted by Balius and published by the Friends of Durruti.

February 1, 1938: *El Amigo del Pueble* No. 12.

July to September 1939: *L'Espagne Nouvelle* Nos. 7 to 9.

Notes to Chapter I

1. The most important studies of the Friends of Durruti Group are: Francisco Manuel Aranda: "Les amis de Durruti" in *Cahiers Leon Trotsky* No. 10 (1982); Jordi Arquer: *Història de la fundació i actuació de la "Agrupación Amigos de Durruti"* Unpublished; Georges Fontenis: *Le message révolutionnaire des "Amis de Durruti"* (Editions L, Paris, 1983); Frank Mintz and Manuel Peciña: *Los Amigos de Durruti, los trotsquistas y los sucesos de mayo* (Campo Abierto, Madrid, 1978); Paul Sharkey: *The Friends of Durruti: A Chronology* (Editorial Crisol, Tokyo, May 1984)

2. According to an affidavit by Jaume Anton Aiguadér, nephew of Artemi Aiguadér, signed in the presence of witnesses in Mexico City on August 9, 1946: "At the time of the May events, the Generalidad government asked for aircraft from Spain in order to bomb the CNT buildings and the latter refused the request." This statement is borne out by the teletype messages exchanged between Companys and the central government. In those messages, on Tuesday, May 4, 1937, the Generalidad President informed the cabinet under-secretary that the rebels had brought artillery out on to the streets, and he asked that Lieutenant-Colonel Felipe Diaz Sandino, commander of the Prat de Lllobregat military air base, be instructed to place himself at the disposal of the Generalidad government: "Generalidad President informs cabinet under-secretary that rebels have brought cannons on to streets. Asks that Sandino be ordered place himself disposal of Generalidad government." [Documentation on deposit in the Hoover Institution.]

3. According to the testimony of Diego Abad de Santillán.

2. Towards July 19

In the elections of February 16, 1936, which the Popular Front won by a narrow margin, the anarchists mounted only token propaganda on behalf of their abstentionist principles and watchwords. According to their revolutionary analysis of the situation, the anarcho-syndicalist leadership took the view that confrontation with the military and with the fascists was inevitable, no matter how the elections might turn out.[1] So they set about making serious preparations for an imminent revolutionary insurrection.

The "Nosotros" group, made up of Francisco Ascaso, Buenaventura Durruti, Juan Garcia Oliver, Aurelio Fernandez, Ricardo Sanz, Gregorio Jover, Antonio Ortiz and Antonio Martinez "Valencia," set itself up as a Central Revolutionary Defense Committee. Members of the "Nosotros" group were men of action, who wielded undeniable working class sway over the CNT masses. In the early morning of July 19, 1936, these men climbed into lorries full of armed militants and slowly toured the working class Pueblo Nuevo district en route to the city center. They put into effect the libertarian practice of teaching by example. The factory sirens issued a summons to workers' insurrection. What few weapons were available to them had been obtained in October 1934, gathered up from the streets where they had been dumped by the Catalanists, or amassed in the weeks leading up to July 19th in raids on armories, police, military depots, ships' arsenals, etc. There were a lot more militants than weapons, and for every combatant downed there was another three to squabble over his rifle or handgun. But the bulk of the weaponry had been captured in the course of street-fighting. The revolt of the soldiery and the fascists became an insurrectionary uprising when the people, following the storming of the San Andres barracks, seized some 35,000 rifles. The workers had successfully armed themselves. It was this that lay behind the resignation of Escofet, the Generalidad Commissar for Public Order. It was important for the Republican Left of Catalonia (ERC) and for the Generalidad government that the army revolt be crushed: but this arming of the people was an augury of a horrible disaster, more to be feared than a fascist victory.[2]

> Thanks to its militants' class instinct, the CNT not only managed to defeat the army revolt but ensured the success of a proletarian uprising. But when something more than class instinct was required, when implementation of revolutionary theory was required, everything went to pot. No Revolutionary Theory, No Revolution. And the very protagonists of the success of the workers' uprising were startled to find the revolution slipping from their grasp.

We are not about to rehearse the deeds, nor the tactical acumen which made the success of the popular uprising in Barcelona feasible. Here all that concerns us is to emphasize that the "Nosotros" group (abetted by other FAI affinity groups) acted as a revolutionary vanguard astute enough to steer the confederal masses towards a victorious uprising. We are also concerned to underline the inability of that group, and of all the labor leaders and organizations, anarchist or otherwise, to consolidate the revolution, when power was within their grasp and was there for the taking, because one may be armed with a rifle but disarmed in political terms. How are we to account for, how are we to understand the undisputed leaders of the CNT trotting along to a rendezvous with Companys in the Generalidad Palace? How could they have heeded a man who **in the early morning** of July 19th refused the CNT weapons, and who had so often harassed and incarcerated them? How come there was still a government in the Generalidad? Why did they not march up to the Generalidad and do away with the bourgeoisie's government? How come they did not proclaim libertarian communism?[3]

The unaccustomed speed of events, the rapidly shifting situations, features of any revolutionary era, took but a few months to turn rebels into ministers, revolutionaries into advocates of "softly, softly," Stalinists into butchers, Catalanists into supplicants before the central government, anarchists into loyal allies and staunch bulwarks of the State, POUMists into victims of a brutal and hitherto inconceivable political repression, socialists into hostages to Stalinism and the Friends of Durruti into mavericks and provocateurs.

Again we stress that we have no intention of rehearsing events here, because there are already books available from a number of writers and a variety of political outlooks, and to these we would refer anyone who is keen to learn, explore or review the concrete historical facts.[4] Our concern here is with discovering, explaining and unveiling the mechanism by which anarchists were turned into ministers, anti-militarists into soldiery, enemies of the State into collaborators with the State and genuine revolutionaries tried and tested in a thousand battles into unwitting stalwarts of counterrevolution.

Our real preoccupation is with explaining the phenomenon which plunged so many revolutionary militants into confusion and the paradox of believing that they were defending the revolution when in reality they were acing as the vanguard of counterrevolution. And to that end, we must first set out the theoretical points[5] which afford us an insight into and which reveal the nature of the historical process initiated (in Catalonia especially) in July 1936:

1. Without destruction of the State, there is no revolution. The Central Anti-fascist Militias Committee of Catalonia (CAMC)[6] was not an organ of dual power, but an agency for military mobilization of the workers, for sacred union with the bourgeoisie, in short, an agency of class collaboration.
2. Arming of the people is meaningless. The nature of military warfare is determined by the nature of the class directing it. An army fighting in defense of a bourgeois State, even should it be antifascist, is an army in the service of capitalism.
3. War between a fascist State and an antifascist State is not a revolutionary class war. The proletariat's intervention on one side is an indication that it has already been defeated. Insuperable technical and professional inferiority on the part of the popular or militia-based army was implicit in military struggle on a military front.
4. War on the military fronts implied abandonment of the class terrain. Abandonment of the class struggle signified defeat for the revolutionary process.
5. In the Spain of August 1936, revolution was no more and there was scope only for war: A nonrevolutionary military war.
6. The collectivizations and socializations in the economy count for nothing when State power is in the hands of the bourgeoisie.

Secondly, attention needs to be drawn to the Gordian knot which loomed as a dilemma in the week following July 19: either the capitalist State would be swept away, and the proletariat would step the class struggle up a gear with the introduction of libertarian communism and the launching of a revolutionary war, or the capitalist State would be allowed to rebuild its apparatus of rule.

Thirdly, there is room to ask why the revolutionary option was not exercised. And the answer is very simple: there was no revolutionary vanguard capable of steering the revolution.

In a logical, stringent, precise and telling way, these theses on the Spanish revolutionary and counterrevolutionary process account for and shed light upon many individual and collective performances, which otherwise strike us as absurd, inexplicable or stubbornly wrong-headed — for instance — the summoning of the CNT leaders to a meeting with Companys in the Generalidad Palace on July 21; a CNT-plenum's acceptance of collaboration with the Generalidad government; the formation and winding-up of the CAMC: the entry of CNT militants into the Generalidad government, the militarization of the militias: the entry into the Republican government of anarcho-syndicalist ministers: the immediate endorsement by these new "anarchist ministers" of the government's flight from Madrid: the cooperation of anarcho-syndicalist leaders in the putting down of the workers' uprising in May 1937: the CNT-UGT unity compact of 1938: collaboration with the Negrin government, etc.

Notes for Chapter 2.

1. See Garcia Oliver's answers (which date from the first half of 1950) to a questionnaire from Burnett Bolloten [on deposit with the Hoover Institution]: "With regard to the February elections, the CNT-FAI adopted the following line, which was peddled throughout Spain at rallies as well as in writing. ***The forthcoming elections are going to be decisive for the Spanish people. If the working class votes for the left, the latter will take power, but we will have to confront an uprising by the military and the right aimed at seizing power. If the working class does not vote for the left, that would spell a lawful success for fascism. We for our part advise the working class to do as it pleases with regard to voting, but we say to it, that if it does not vote for the left, before six month will have elapsed from the later's victory, we shall have to resist the fascist right with weapons in hand.*** Naturally, Spain's working class, which had for many years been advised by the CNT not to vote, placed upon our propaganda the construction we wanted, which is to say, that

it should vote, in that it would always be better to stand up to the fascist right, if they revolted, once defeated and out of government. The left won in the February 1936 elections. Companys became the government in Catalonia and the left became the government of Spain. We had honored our commitments, ***but they honored none of theirs, in that they issued not one weapon, nor did they take any preemptive action against the fascist military plot.***"

2. See the exchange between Companys and Escofet in the wake of the crushing of the fascists' rebellion:

"Mr President" — I said to him — "I bring you official word that the rebellion has been completely defeated [. . .]"

"Good, Escofet, very good" — the President replied — "But the situation is chaotic. Uncontrolled armed riffraff have invaded the streets and are committing all sorts of outrages. And anyway, the CNT, heavily armed, is master of the city. What can we do against them?"

"For the time being, we have all been swept along, including the CNT leaders themselves. The only solution, Mr President, is to contain the situation politically, without letting any of our respective authorities go by the board. If you, for your part, can succeed in that, I undertake to take charge of Barcelona whenever you order me so to do or when circumstances permit." [Federico Escofet: *De una derrota a una victoria : 6 de octubre de 1934–19 de julio de 1936* (Ed. Argos-Vergara, Barcelona, 1984, p. 352)]

3. Garcia Oliver addresses many of these questions directly or indirectly in his account of the interview with Companys: "The military-fascist uprising had come just as we had predicted. Companys retreated into the Police Headquarters in Barcelona, where I saw him at, it must have been, seven in the morning on July 19, terrified of the consequences of what he could see coming, in that he anticipated that, once all of the troop regiments in Barcelona had revolted, they would easily sweep aside all resistance. However, almost single-handedly, the CNT-FAI forces held out for those two memorable days, and after an epic and bitter struggle [. . .] we defeated all the regiments [. . .] For all these reasons, Companys was bewildered and shocked to find the CNT-FAI's representatives before him. Bewildered because all he could think about was the heavy responsibility he had with regard to us and the Spanish people because of his failure to heed all our forecasts. [. . .] Shocked, because although they had not honored the commitments they had given us, the CNT-FAI in Barcelona and in Catalonia had beaten the rebels [. . .] So, when he sent for us, Companys told us: "I know that you have lots of grounds for complaint and annoyance where I am concerned. I have opposed you greatly and failed to appreciate you for what you are. However, it is never too late for an honest apology and mine, which I am now going to offer you, is tantamount to a confession: had I appreciated

your worth, maybe the circumstances now would be different; but it is too late for that now, and you alone have defeated the rebel military and in all logic you ought to govern. If that is your view, I gladly surrender the Generalidad Presidency to you, and, if you think that I can be of any assistance elsewhere, you need only tell me the place I should take up. ***But if, since we do not yet know for sure who has had the victory elsewhere in Spain, you believe that I may still be of service in acting as Catalonia's lawful representative from the Generalidad presidency, say so, and from there, and always with your agreement, we shall carry on this fight until it becomes clear who are the winners.***" For our part, and this was the CNT-FAI's view, we held that Companys should stay on as head of the Generalidad, precisely because we had not taken to the streets to fight specifically for the social revolution, but rather to defend ourselves against the fascist mutiny." [From Garcia Oliver's 1950 answers to Bolloten's questionnaire, on deposit at the Hoover Institution.]

Garcia Oliver's testimony deserves to be set alongside that of Federica Montseny: "In no one's wildest imaginings, not even those of Garcia Oliver, the most Bolshevik of us all, did the idea of taking revolutionary power arise. It was later, when the scale of the upheaval and the people's initiatives became plain, that there began to be debate about whether or not we should go for broke." [Abel Paz: *Durruti: El proletariado en armas* (Bruguera, Barcelona, 1978, pp. 381-382)]

4. Among the most interesting of these are the anarchist Abel Paz (*Durruti: El proletariado en armas)*, the Civil Guard Francisco Lacruz (*El alzamiento, la revolución y el terror en Barcelona*), the book, cited above, by Escofet, the Generalidad's commissar for public order, and the memoirs of Abad de Santillán and Garcia Oliver. As for standard texts, we simply cannot fail to mention Burnett Bolloten *La Guerra civil española: Revolución y contrarrevolución* (Alianza Editorial, Madrid, 1989) and Pierre Broue *Staline et la revolution. Le cas espagnol* (Fayard, Paris, 1993).

5. And which are of course the expression of a given *political viewpoint*, which may or may not be shared, but which we set out plainly here for what it is, without pretending to or invoking any nonexistent, hackneyed ***academic objectivity.***

6. And the People's Executive Committee in Valencia or the Defense Committee in Madrid.

EL AMIGO DEL PUEBLO

PORTAVOZ DE LOS AMIGOS DE DURRUTI

Año I • Núm. 3 • 20 Céntimos • Redacción y Administración: Rambla de las Flores, 1 • Teléfono 18721 • Barcelona, Sábado, 12 de Junio de 1937

EDITORIAL

Una hora Histórica

UNA VEZ MAS

Maniobras contra-revolucionarias

EN TORNO DE LAS JORNADAS DE MAYO

3. From July to May: Uncontrollables or Revolutionaries?

The gestation of May 1937 began one week after the revolutionary events of July 1936.

In Catalonia, the revolutionary uprising of the working masses had successfully defeated the military, thrown the State's administrative and repressive machinery into disarray and removed the bourgeois class from its leadership functions. Not only had the military rising against the Republic been frustrated, but the capitalist State itself had succumbed. The Catalan working class seized weapons from the barracks it had stormed, ensured that the repressive agencies fraternized with the people in arms and introduced a new, revolutionary order[1]: it organized and directed production inside firms, which were either collectivized or socialized: and set up People's Militias, which set off for Aragon.

Power was in the streets. The people was armed. But no proletarian organization assumed power. The working class retained its trade union and political organizations, without creating new organs of (unified) workers' power. And that is not all. In order to keep afloat the spectral, discredited and impotent bourgeois Generalidad government, which was melting like a sugar-cube, the so-called Central Antifascist Militias Committee (CAMC) was established. **At no time** was the CAMC ever the embryo of a new workers' power: it was, rather, a class collaboration agency,[2] a provisional government that helped to restore the power of the bourgeois, republican

Generalidad. The CAMC supplanted the Generalidad government in those functions — relative to the army, public order and production — which there was no one else capable of performing, following the disintegration of bourgeois institutions. President Company's power was merely nominal, but it was also the *potential* power of the capitalist State, which anarchists not merely allowed to subsist but actually helped to survive and resurrect itself, allowing it to "legalize," post facto, the revolutionary gains made during the events in July. Without looking for it, the CAMC acquired all of the accoutrements of a government. But instead of centralizing the revolutionary power of the committees — local committees, defense committees, workers' committees, peasants' committees and committees of every sort — it became the chief impediment to their unification and reinforcement. The CAMC was a life-jacket tossed to a Generalidad awash in a sea of local revolutionary committees, isolated from one another, which in Catalonia wielded the only real power between July 19 and September 26.[3]

At no point was there a dual power situation in existence. This notion is *crucial* to any understanding of the Spanish revolution and civil war. The CAMC was a class collaborationist agency. It was not the germ of workers' power **at loggerheads** with the power of the capitalist State. And this was obvious to all the main political leaders,[4] whether or not participants in the CAMC. For this reason, the dissolution of the CAMC was not a traumatic event, nor unduly important: it was just one of many steps in the process of reconstructing the State power, dismantled and battered after the July events. The formation of the new Generalidad government, with the CNT and the POUM being incorporated into it, was the logical *sequel* to the work carried out by the various parties and trade unions within the CAMC.

This counterrevolutionary process, this process of reconstruction of capitalist State power necessarily spawned a number of contradictions, and naturally was camouflaged or covered up by the CNT's leading cadres with the familiar "circumstancialist" arguments invoking antifascist unity, the need to win the war, the CNT's being a minority elsewhere in Spain, the dangers of scandalizing the western democracies, etc. Or even the most naive argument — that they were *turning away* from an "anarchist dictatorship."

For the CNT, the chief contradiction in this unstoppable reconquest of all of the capitalist State's proper functions, lay in the fact that this was feasible only at the cost of an equally continuous and irreversible loss of the "gains" which the masses had won in July.

Between December 1936 and May 1937, we witness a tug of war and a growing tension between constant concessions by the CNT, marginalization of the POUM, the Generalidad's insatiable pressure to recover all of its functions, and the overbearing pressures from the Soviets and their infiltration into the State apparatuses, in Catalonia and in the central government alike.

It was for that reason that the Control Patrols, and everything having to do with public order, border control and communications, were in the eye of the hurricane. For revolutionary militants, labeled "uncontrollables" in the terminology of their adversaries, retention of control over public order, the borders and communications and, of course, the existence of the Control Patrols were the basic threshold marking the point of no return in the unceasing concessions by the CNT leadership.

The revolutionary insurrection of July 1936 had been based on the district or local Defense Committees set up and trained many months in advance.[5] In the wake of the July events, the Control Patrols were afforded "legal" recognition as a revolutionary police answerable to the CAMC.

But the Control Patrols did not account for the whole of the insurrectionist movement. There were also all these district or local Defense Committees and other groups and militants. Furthermore, we need to underline the radically different natures of the Control Patrols and the Defense Committees. The Control Patrols were an organization created by the CAMC, to which they owed their organization, orders and manpower. The Defense Committees were a CNT insurgent agency, in existence from well before July 1936. The Control Patrols were the *institutionalization* of the success of the workers' uprising; the Defense Committees, converted into Revolutionary Committees, which led a vegetative existence between July 1936 and May 1937, represented the *insurrectionist movement.*[6] Hence the attacks by all political forces, including the CNT-FAI and POUM, upon the so-called "uncontrollables."

This derogatory label fitted comfortably with facile highlighting of outrages and abuses by a few delinquents. But the charge also targeted the CNT and the measure of its "control" over its own membership. Indeed, in the newspapers — not excepting the confederal press, the vast majority of which supposed collaborationism — the term "uncontrollable" was used as a synonym for criminal. This implication was unremarkable in the bourgeois or Stalinist press, because they regarded revolutionaries as criminals. The serious paradox was when the CNT or the POUM used the idea of "uncontrollable" to excuse abandonment of their own ideological principles.

In every revolutionary process, there arise groups or individuals who utilize force of arms for their own advantage. But this minority can quickly and easily be subdued by a consolidated workers' power, as the Russian case demonstrates. In the Catalan case, it is apparent that the attack on the "uncontrollables" is almost always an attack upon proletarian justice (alien to bourgeois legality) and on revolutionaries, which is to say, on those refusing to let go of the gains secured by the proletariat in the July uprising, or indeed, keen to take them "further."[7]

Let us caution the reader that this approach presupposes a very particular political option[8] that examines and accounts for the events, ideologies and contradictions of the Spanish revolution of 1936-1939 in terms of the consequence of the non-existence of a revolutionary party.

Naturally, the term "uncontrollable" was not, and even today, is not employed as an innocent, neutral term. It is absolutely a derogatory, class term, through which the bourgeoisie was trying to discredit and defame revolutionaries. It is no accident that in May 1937 the Friends of Durruti were obliged to hear themselves insulted as uncontrollables as well as agents provocateurs and mavericks, even by the FAI itself. Their only offense was to have attempted to present revolutionary goals to the proletariat fighting on the barricades.

In every historical narrative, there is always an option in favor of a particular political assumption. Very rarely is it explicit, and it is virtually always denied and hidden, in favor of a supposed "objectivity" which is both sublimated and nonexistent.[9]

One final observation: May 1937 signaled the final defeat of the revolutionary process launched in July 1936. But it was not the end of the process of counterrevolution, nor the end of CNT collaborationism, which would culminate in the conclusion of the CNT-UGT pact in March–April 1938 and in entry into the Negrin government.

Notes for Chapter 3

1. See Balius's arguments: "the establishment of committees of workers, peasants, militians and sailors was an instantaneous reaction to the destruction of the capitalist machinery of coercion. There was not a single factory, working class district, village, militias battalion or vessel where a committee was not set up. The committee was the ultimate authority, whose ordinances and agreements had to be abided by. Its justice, revolutionary justice, to the exclusion of every other (. . .) the only law was the imperious requirements of the revolution. Most of the committees were democratically elected by the workers, militians, sailors and peasants, regardless of denomination, thereby representing proletarian democracy, superseding a treacherous bourgeois parliamentary democracy. In short, there was but one power in the workplace: labor and the workers.
Generally, expropriation of the bourgeoisie and landowners was carried out as the committees were established (. . .) there was a similar transfer of powers with regard to arms. (. . .) Militias were set up (. . .) Control patrols were founded to see to the maintenance of the nascent, new revolutionary order (. . .)

The Spanish proletariat's answer (. . .) was highly categorical and intelligent. The reaction had been crushed on the streets and expropriated economically, and the proletariat set itself up as the country's arbiter (. . .)"
(Jaime Balius "Recordando julio de 1936" in *Le Combat syndicaliste* of April 1, 1971) [This article by Balius lifts whole sentences, word for word, from pages 292-294 of G. Munis's book *Jalones de derrota, promesa de victoria* (Zero, Bilbao, 1977)]
2. See, for instance, the sharp and radical alternative posited by Garcia Oliver: "Between social revolution and the Militias' Committee, the Organization plumped for the Militias Committee." (Juan Garcia Oliver *El eco de los pasos* Ruedo Ibérico, Paris-Barcelona, 1978, p. 188)
3. Munis contends that after the July events all that remained was the governing power of the committees: "If the situation in the weeks following July 19 is to be characterized more precisely, it has to be defined as power diffused into the hands of the proletariat and the peasants. These were fully cognizant of their local power, although they lacked appreciation of the need to coordinate their power across the country. For its part, during those first weeks, the bourgeois Government lacked the capacity and will to combat the nascent workers' power. There can be no talk of duality until later, when the Popular Front government came to, realized that it had survived, marshaled around itself whatever armed forces it could muster and set about contesting power with the committees of the proletariat and peasants." (G. Munis "Significado histórico del 19 de julio" in *Contra la corriente* No. 6, Mexico, August 1943.)
We shall not here enter into analysis of the dual power thesis advanced by Munis for the period following July 19, 1936, which is to say, for the period between early October 1936 and May 1937. The difference between the position of the Italian Fraction and Munis's position resides in the fact that the Bordiguists reckoned that, in the absence of utter destruction of the capitalist State, there can be no talk of revolution, whereas Munis took the line that the bourgeois State had been momentarily eclipsed. We simply point out the discrepancy and shall delve no further into the issue. What we are concerned to indicate here is the role played by the CAMC as a class collaborationist agency.
4. This has been explicitly stated by, among others, figures as prominent and simultaneously so politically divergent as Garcia Oliver, Nin, Tarradellas, Azaña and Balius himself. See especially Nin's article "El problema de los órganos de poder en la revolución espanola," published in French in *Juillet. Rvue internationale du POUM* No. 1, Barcelona-Paris, June 1937.
5. See Juan Garcia Oliver *El movimiento libertario en España* (2) Colección de Historia Oral. Fundación Salvador Segui, Madrid, undated.
6. See the detailed description offered by Abel Paz: *Viaje al pasado (1936–1939)* (Ed. del Autor, Barcelona, 1995, pp. 63-64):

> The Defense Committees which, with the army coup attempt, had turned into Revolutionary Committees, once the Central Antifascist Militias Committee of Catalonia had been launched, had ignored the latter's authority and their activities had led to a local orchestration, based in the Casa CNT-FAI itself, making these committees a power within the power of the CNT-FAI higher committees; but they were a real power, greater even than the power of the higher committees. Each district committee had its own defense groups at its disposal. Groups comprised an indeterminate membership that could oscillate between six and ten. Every one of these comrades had a rifle and even a pistol kept permanently in his care. The Clot district, where I operated, boasted 15 defense groups, which, at a conservative estimate, meant around a hundred rifles. But to this strength must be added the factory groups, with their roots in the Clot district; these too had their own defense groups with their own weapons, up to and including machine-guns. Finally, the Libertarian Youth groups and anarchist groups also had to be included. This motley assortment was the material with which our district's Defense Committee had to work.

7. See, for instance, Garcia Oliver's threatening and contemptuous snubbing of Companys when the latter called at the CACM headquarters on July 25th to register a protest at the civil disorder and the activities of uncontrollables, in Juan Garcia Oliver *El Eco de los Pasos* op. cit. pp. 193-194.
8. As spelled out in the thesis on the nature of the revolution and the Spanish civil war set out in Chapter 2 of this edition (No. 3) of *Balance*. See also No. 1 of *Balance*, which examines the theses of the Italian Fraction (Bordiguists) on the Spanish civil war.
9. See the defamatory remarks about the Catalan anarchist movement and the allegations made against Jaime Balius or Antonio Martin, who are depicted as savage ogres by H. Raguer, J.M. Solé and J. Villarroya, who espouse a "neutrality" which is bourgeois, sanctimonious and Catalanist. See, for instance, the utterly extravagant accusations, dissevered from the context of a revolutionary situation proper, leveled at Balius on pages 256-258 of the book by the Benedictine friar H. Raguer *Divendres de passió. Vida i mort de Carrasco i Formiguera* (Pub. Abadia Montserrat, Barcelona, 1984) and on pages 67 and 68 of *La repressió a la reraguarda de Catalunya (1936-1939)* (Pub. Abadia Montserrat, Barcelona, 1989) by J.M. Solé Sabate and J. Villarroya Font. Also worth mentioning is a little volume offering a Catalanist version of the anarchist government of Cerdañia, which involved complete anarchist control of the border with France, and of the bloody incidents in Belver, (a direct prece-

dent of the May Events in Barcelona), following which the Generalidad government managed to capture absolute control in that border region. See J. Pons i Porta and J.M. Solé i Sabate *Anarquia i Republica a la Cerdanya (1936-1939) El "Cojo de Málaga" i els fets de Bellver* (Pub. Abadia Montserrat, Barcelona, 1991). It has to be stressed that all of these books have been published by the publishing house of the Montserrat Monastery, which of course suggests plain ideological servility, which we refuse to accept as valid in any "objective" evaluation of Jaime Balius and Antonio Martin, much less their constant delirium, defamation and prejudices with regard to the libertarian movement. See too the nonsense and outrageous remarks about Balius, and the derogatory remarks about the libertarian movement, uttered from a pedantic, academic perspective, incapable of comprehending the meaning in the 1930s of an action group, a trade union, a workers' athenaeum or a general strike, in the article "Grupos de afinidad, disciplina belica y periodismo libertario, 1936-1938" by Susana Tavera and Enric Ucelay da Cal, in *História Contemporánea* No. 9, (Servicio Ed. Universidad del Pais Vasco, 1993)
By contrast, well worth reading are Josep Eduard Adsuar's interesting and illuminating articles on the libertarian movement. See, for example, "El Comitè Central de Milicies Antifeixistes" in *L'Avenç* No. 14 (March 1979), "La fascinación del poder: Diego Abad de Santillán en el ojo del huracán" in *Anthropos* No. 138 (November 1992). Very interesting too are articles by Anna Monjo and Carme Vega in the review *Historia Oral* No. 3, (1990): "Clase obrera y guerra civil" and "Socialización y Hechos de Mayo," and, of course, *Els treballadors i la guerre civil. Historia d'una indústria catalana colectivitzada* by Anna Monjo and Carme Vega ((Empuries, Barcelona, 1986)

4. Origins of the Friends of Durruti. The Opposition to Militarization and Balius's Journalistic Career

The Friends of Durruti Group was formally launched on March 17, 1937, although its origins can be traced back to October 1936. The Group was the confluence of two main currents: the opposition on the part of anarchist militians from the Durruti Column (and the Iron Column[1]) to militarization of the people's militias, and the opposition to governmentalism, best articulated in the writings of Jaime Balius (though not Jaime Balius only) in *Solidaridad Obrera* between July and November 1936, in *Ideas*, between December 1936 and April 1937, and in *La Noche* between March and May 1937.

Both currents, the "militia" current repudiating militarization of the people's militias, as represented by Pablo Ruiz, and the "journalistic" critique of the CNT-FAI's collaboration with the government, as spearheaded by Jaime Balius, opposed the CNT's circumstantialist ideology (which provided the alibi for the jettisoning of anarchism's quintessential and fundamental characteristics) as embodied, to varying degrees, by Federica Montseny, Garcia Oliver, Abad de Santillán or Juan Peiro, among others.

Repudiation of militarization of the People's Militias caused grave unease in several anarchist militia units, and was articulated at the plenum of confederal and anarchist columns held in Valencia from February 5 to 8,

1937.[2] Pablo Ruiz attended as delegate from the Durruti Column's militians of the Gelsa sector who were resistant to militarization, and Francisco Pellicer[3] was present to represent the militians of The Iron Column. The Gelsa sector even witnessed a defiant refusal to comply with the orders received from the CNT and FAI Regional Committees that militarization be accepted. The acrimony between those Durruti Column militians who agreed to the militarization and those who rejected it caused serious problems, leading in the end to the formation of a commission from the Column, headed by Manzana, which raised the problem with the Regional Committee. The upshot of these discussions was the decision that all militians be given a fortnight to choose one of two courses of action: accept the militarization imposed by the Republican government, or quit the front.[4]

Balius's journalistic trajectory between July 1936 and the end of the war is very telling. His political stance of advocacy of permanent revolution remained virtually unchanged whereas his professional and personal standing underwent rapid change with the incoming tide of counterrevolution.

Between July and early November 1936, Balius, who, with no help other than his friend Gilabert, saw to it that *Solidaridad Obrera* hit the streets on July 20,[5] published numerous articles in that paper, the chief organ of the CNT. Some were purely informative[6] in character, as was appropriate for journalistic reportage: but many of them, and without doubt the most interesting among them, were expressions of political opinion. These articles, which filled a regular column in *Solidaridad Obrera*,[7] occasionally appeared on the cover by way of editorial comment by the paper.[8] And there is every likelihood that Balius was the writer of several editorials (in September-October 1936), published without byline[9] as expressions of the *Solidaridad Obrera* policy line. But whatever the extent of his involvement in the drafting of these editorials, it can be affirmed beyond doubt of any sort that Balius, through the pages of the CNT's organ in Catalonia, in September and October 1936, during Liberto Callejas's time as managing editor, played a very prominent ideological role as molder and shaper of the political stance of the CNT's main daily newspaper. Ever present in his articles was insistence upon defense of the revolutionary gains of July and the need to press these home to which end he urged tough, decisive repressive measures or, as Balius liked to call them, invoking the French Revolution, "public safety" measures against the counterrevolutionary threat from the bourgeoisie.[10]

At the beginning of November 1936, Liberto Callejas was stood down as managing editor of *Solidaridad Obrera*. Jacinto Toryho was appointed in his place.[11] Bear in mind that at the beginning of November Durruti had gone to the Madrid front and four confederal ministers had joined the

Republican government. Toryho's appointment was in response to the need for the director of *Solidaridad Obrera* to be an adamant champion of the CNT's circumstantialist and collaborationist policy. By the end of December, Toryho had managed to get rid of Liberto Callejas's old editorial team of Jaime Balius, Mingo, Alejandro Gilabert, Pintado, Galipienzo, Borras, Gamón,[12] etc., who were against the official CNT policy, and their place was taken by contributions from prominent anarcho-syndicalist leaders such as Peiró, Montseny and Abad de Santillán, faithful friends of Toryho, such as Leandro Blanco (erstwhile editor of a monarchist newspaper) and the prestigious bylines of "progressives" like Cánovas Cervantes and Zamacois.[13]

One of the last articles Balius published in *Solidaridad Obrera* (on December 6, 1936) under the title "Durruti's testament," is deserving of a detailed mention. The article is a commentary upon the radio broadcast made by Durruti from Madrid on November 5,[14] only days before he died: written in what might have appealed to many anarchists a provocative manner, this article gives us an inkling of what was to become one of the basic ideological pillars of the future Friends of Durruti Group, namely, the *totalitarian* character of any proletarian revolution:

> Durruti bluntly stated that we anarchists require that the revolution be of a totalitarian nature. And that the comrades standing up to fascism so doggedly on the fields of battle are not prepared to let anyone tamper with the revolutionary and liberating import of this present hour.
>
> (. . .) Durruti's testament lives on. It lingers with even greater force than on the night he harangued us. We shall see to it that his last wishes are made a reality.

December 29, 1936 saw the appearance of the first issue of *Ideas* the mouthpiece of the CNT federation in the Bajo Llobregat comarca. Balius had an article published in virtually every edition of *Ideas*. His articles insistently denounced the advance of the counterrevolution.[15] Outstanding among them was the attack upon the President of the Generalidad, Luis Companys, which was carried in *Ideas* No. 15 of April 8, 1937, under the title "Let's make revolution."[16]

Ideas was a direct antecedent of *El Amigo del Pueblo*. Although not every contributor to *Ideas*[17] was a member of the Friends of Durruti, we can state that, along with *Acracia* in Lerida,[18] *Ideas* was the most outstanding mouthpiece of the anarchist revolutionary current prior to May.

Balius was appointed director of *La Noche* on January 26, 1937 by the Local Federation of Unions. *La Noche* was an evening daily, run by a cooperative of workers, most of whom belonged to the CNT, although it was not part of the *organizational* press of the CNT.

It was in *La Noche* of March 2, 1937 that the first report came of the aims and membership conditions of a new anarchist grouping which had taken the name of the "Friends of Durruti Group."[19] Between early March and the May events, *La Noche*, while it never became the Group's official mouthpiece, became, thanks to its not being an organizational paper, the paper in which the Friends of Durruti were able to give free expression to their criticisms of the official policy of the CNT.

Without doubt the most outstanding articles are those from Balius, but we cannot fail to mention those above the signature of Mingo, on the subject of the Municipality and trade union management of the economy, because these represent a very significant factor in the political theory of the Friends of Durruti.

In the March 2, 1937 edition, Balius published an article entitled "Careful, workers, Not a single step backwards," which had the merit of catching the eye of Nin, who, in the March 4th edition of *La Batalla*, gave a glowing welcome to the views set out by Balius, and also to the launching of the Friends of Durruti Group announced in the same edition, on account of the chances that it might give a revolutionary fillip to the CNT masses, whom the anarchist leaders were leading down the path of the crassest and most short-sighted reformism.

In that article, Balius railed against the view, increasingly widespread in some anarchist circles, that, if the war was to be won, the revolution had to be abjured. And he bluntly cited an article signed by the prominent *treintista* militant Juan Peiró. After noting the onslaught of counterrevolution, which was now demanding that the Control Patrols be disbanded, he placed the blame for this upon the ongoing policy of appeasement pursued by the CNT. The article called for an amendment of this policy, for only if the revolution made headway in the rearguard could the war be won on the battle-fronts. The article's title, "Not a single step backwards!" was therefore a very telling one.

On March 6, 1937, Balius had an article in *La Noche* entitled "Counterrevolutionary Postures. Neutral positions are damaging," in which he catalogued the features of the new security force set up by the Generalidad government, identifying it as a bourgeois corps in the service of the capitalist State and inimical to the most elementary interests of the workers.

March 8, 1937 saw the publication in *La Noche* of one of those articles so typical of Balius's style, where, through an astute admixture of news and opinion, he recorded the spectacle of trains crammed with residents of Barcelona off into the countryside in search of foodstuffs. By means of a description of the folk thronging the carriages, Balius lashed out at the new approach being adopted in the provision of supplies, an approach introduced by the Stalinist leader, Comorera.

In its March 11, 1937 edition, *La Noche* carried an article paying tribute to the figure of Durruti. Balius recalled the address given by Durruti over the radio from the Madrid front just days before he died, an address in which he had deplored the failures of the rearguard to take the war to its heart. The solution, as Durruti saw it, lay in waging war properly, enrolling the bourgeois into fortification battalions and placing all workers on a war footing. According to Balius, Durruti's death had been followed by a funeral fit for a king, but no one had taken his reasoning to heart. As a result, the journalist concluded, the argument was beginning to be heard that the civil war was a war of independence and not the class war that Durruti had called for. Balius closed the article by asserting that Durruti was more relevant than ever, and that there could be no loyalty to his memory that did not include subscription to his ideas.

The following day, March 12, Balius had a piece in *La Noche* entitled "Comments by Largo Caballero: Counter-revolution on the march," in which he was critical of statements by the UGT leader, describing them as counterrevolutionary, in that they confirmed an intention to revert to the situation which had obtained prior to July 19, with the collectivizations and socializations of firms being dismantled just as soon as the war was won.

In *La Noche* of March 13, 1937, Balius had an article entitled "We must wage war. Our future requires it," calling for a war economy and criticizing the Generalidad's economic policy.

Balius's article, "Fascist barbarism. We must use the mailed fist" (in *La Noche* of March 16, 1937) referred to the air raids on Barcelona, attacked the exchanges of refugees through the embassies and called for the stamping out of the fifth column. He even recommended that neighborhood watch committees be set up. The writer's conclusion was that an immediate purge of the rearguard was imperative and a necessary prerequisite for success in the war:

> No purge has been made of the rearguard. (. . .) Fascists are still at large in huge numbers. (. . .) Our enemies must be rounded up and eliminated (. . .) Anyone attempting to dampen the fires of popular justice is an enemy of the Revolution. Let us act with the utmost vigor. Heedless of our soft hearts, let us show the mailed fist.

The March 18th edition of *La Noche* carried an insertion reporting the formal launching of the Friends of Durruti. Félix Martin(ez) was listed as the group's secretary and Jaime Balius as vice-secretary. José Paniagua, Antonio Puig, Francisco Carreño, Pablo Ruiz, Antonio Romero, Serafin Sobias and Eduardo Cervera were listed as members of the steering committee.

On Tuesday, March 23, 1937, Balius had a piece published in *La Noche* under the title "Time to be specific: Catalonia's role in the Spanish Revolution," wherein he championed the Catalan proletariat's role as the driving force of a thorough-going social revolution, which was not, as in Madrid and other regions in Spain, hobbled by the immediate needs of the war.

In the March 24th edition, the paper carried a lengthy interview with Pablo Ruiz, a member of the Group and spokesman for the Gelsa militias opposed to militarization of the columns. We are offered a short but intriguing biographical sketch of Pablo Ruiz, thanks to which we know that he was a member of the Figols revolutionary committee back on January 8, 1933, that he fought at the head of forty men in Las Rondas and the Paralelo in the July events, that he had a hand in the siege and final assault upon the Atarazanas barracks, alongside Durruti and Ascaso, and that he had set off for the Aragon front in the Durruti Column, and had been on active service there in the Gelsa sector ever since. After a paean to the virtues and advantages of the anarchist peasant collectivizations in Aragon, the interviewer asks his views on militarization. His answer was considered, prudent and nuanced: but at the same time quite coherent and radical, as if to underline the incompatibility between anarchist ideas and the war's being directed by the bourgeoisie and the Republican State:

> to reorganization of the Army, we have no objection, for it ought to be remembered that we were the first to call for a single, common command (...) in the care of delegates from the various columns by way of ensuring homogeneity in the performance of them all. Let restructuring proceed, but let the people's Army not be in thrall to the Generalidad, nor to the Central Government. It must be under the Confederation's control."

In the interview, Pablo Ruiz alludes to the constant retreat from the revolutionary gains of July and to the inception of the Friends of Durruti:

> When we left for the front we left it to our comrades to ensure that the Revolution would march on to victory, in the anarchist sense. But, in the elaboration of that Revolution, a role has been assigned to the bourgeois parties which had no feeling for the revolution, in that their task was to champion the interests of the petite bourgeoisie and of the UGT which had a very tiny following in Catalonia compared to ours. (...) By entering into

> a compact with them, we have lost hegemony over the Revolution and have found ourselves required to compromise day after day, with the result that the Revolution has been disfigured as the initial revolutionary gains have been whittled away.
>
> Out of this has arisen the formation of the "Friends of Durruti," in that this new organization has as its primary object the preservation, intact, of the postulates of the CNT-FAI.

Pablo Ruiz concluded the interview by setting out his own view of how the revolution might be set back on the right track: 1. Propaganda should be carried out within the CNT, without recourse to violence. 2. There should be pressure for trade union (CNT) direction of the economy. 3. The political parties should be pushed aside. 4. No alliance and no compromise with the forces harboring the counterrevolution, that is, the PSUC and the UGT:

> The direction of the economy and of society ought to be vested in the trade union organization [the CNT], with no place for the political parties, on the basis that these do not meet the criteria to be regarded as renovative. None of which implies imposition through force, but rather through propaganda within CNT ranks. [. . .] And I am opposed to involving the political parties, being convinced that that would entail loss of the revolution, which has to be prosecuted by every means short of compromise with groups that not only have no feeling for the revolution but are also in the minority.

Balius published (in the March 27, 1937 edition *La Noche*) an article entitled "The revolution has its requirements. All power to the unions," in which he dealt with the protracted crisis in the Generalidad government. His view of the trade unions as organs of the revolution is very interesting. He classified the Generalidad government crisis as the product of the tensions characterizing a situation of dual power: the Generalidad made laws and passed decrees, but the unions paid no heed to the Generalidad's decisions. In Balius's view, for the revolution to move forward and consolidate, power had to pass to the working class, and this was encapsulated in the slogan: 'All power to the unions.'

Balius also penned an intriguing article entitled "A historical moment. A categorical dilemma" (*La Noche* April 5, 1937), in which he probed the significance of the crisis in the Generalidad government. As far as Balius was concerned, the Generalidad was a relic from the past, one that was incongruent with the new revolutionary needs:

> The Generalidad government is a hang-over from the past, from a petit-bourgeois system that involves all sorts of incongruencies, vacillation and hypocrisy.

Thus, according to Balius, there could be only one resolution of the Generalidad government crisis. A change of government personnel would achieve nothing. And Balius even made a veiled **appeal for the CNT to replace the Generalidad with the power of the workers, and sweep the counterrevolutionary parties out of existence:**

> We are not pessimists, but we honestly believe that we have not been equal to the challenge.
>
> The dilemma cannot be sidestepped. The future of the proletariat requires heroic decisions. If there are some organizations attempting to strangle the revolution, we must be ready to shoulder the responsibility of a moment in history which, by reason of its very grandeur, presupposes a series of measures and decisions that are not out of tune with the present hour.
>
> **With the Revolution, or lined up against it.** There can be no middle ground.

In *La Noche* of April 7th, Balius had an article entitled "In this grave hour. The sovereign will resides in the people," in which he reiterated the viewpoint he had spelled out in his April 5th article and repeated his attacks on Companys.

Also in *La Noche*, there were several articles by Mingo,[20] remarkable for their vehemence, sounding the alarm about the advance of the counterrevolution, eulogizing anarchism's revolutionary spirit (which was held to be incompatible with governmental collaborationism, which had to be ended forthwith), attacking the UGT, the PSUC, Comorera and Companys over their constant defamation of the Confederation, agreeing that there was an overriding need (as spelled out by Balius) to do away with the Generalidad, and echoing the growing malaise among the people. But the most interesting of these articles was the one given over to the municipalities, because his thinking (merely outlined here) was to be spelled out in full in the program set out by the Friends of Durruti in *El Amigo del Pueblo* after May. In that article,[21] Mingo stated:

> The municipality is the authentic revolutionary government.

According to Mingo, ever since July 19, 1936, the Generalidad government had been redundant. The only policy now was economic policy, and that was the province of the trade unions. So, according to Mingo, the municipality, run by the workers, with economic policy supervised by the workers, could and should have stepped into the shoes of the State.

In the April 14, 1937 edition of the daily *La Noche,* Balius had an article, "A historic date: April 14," marking the anniversary of the proclamation of the Republic, in which he underlined the petit-bourgeois character of the day when the Republic was proclaimed, attacked Catalanism, whether right-wing or left-wing, Macià or Cambó, in that both had forsworn their nationalism in the face of threats from the Catalan proletariat.

Without the slightest doubt, these articles of Balius's, (and of other members of the Friends of Durruti), touching upon such a wide variety of topics, generally political opinion, but also with a news content, were the mortar binding together a critical current of opposition to the CNT's collaborationist policy. Balius was not the sole critic, but he was one of the most outstanding and of course the one most consistent, coherent and radical. Balius's merit resides in his having secured the backing of a sizable group of militians opposed to the militarization of the Militias. The conjunction of these militians, led by Pablo Ruiz, with other anarcho-syndicalists opposed to the CNT's collaborationist policy found its political views articulated in theoretical terms in Balius's articles and criticisms. Those views were to crystallize in the program set out on the poster dating from late April 1937 and would be spelled out in greater detail in *El Amigo del Pueblo* newspaper, published after the May Events.

So, to sum up: although the Friends of Durruti Grouping was formally launched on March 17, 1937, its origins can be traced to the deep-seated malaise created in militians' ranks by the Generalidad decree on militarization of the People's Militias, which is to say, to late October 1936, when Durruti was still alive. Then again, Balius had come to prominence as early as 1935 as a journalist and anarchist ideologue, known for his interesting theoretical contributions on nationalism, his savage criticisms of the Catalan bourgeoisie's political activities, his attacks on Macià and Companys, his expose of the Catalanist fascism embodied in Dencas and Badia, as well as his analysis of the events of October 1934 in Catalonia from a CNT perspective. Nor was collaboration between Jaime Balius and Pablo Ruiz anything new, since they had jointly written a pamphlet[22] and had both belonged to the same anarchist affinity group, "Renacer" — that being the name of the publishing house which had issued Balius's pamphlets prior to July 1936.[23] In addition to Jaime Balius and Pablo Ruiz, the "Renacer" group included Francisco Pellicer (who would be the Iron Column's delegate during the civil war) and Bruno Lladó (who was a Sabadell city councilor during the war and the Generalidad Department of Economy's comarcal delegate).[24]

Notes for Chapter 4

1. On the Iron Column, see Abel Paz's splendid study *Crònica de la Columna de Ferro* (Hacer, Barcelona, 1984). As early as September and October 1936, the Iron Column had figured in sensational incidents concerned with cleansing the rearguard (Valencia city), traveling there from the front lines in order to demand the disarmament and disbanding of armed corps in the service of the State and the despatching of their members to front-line service. Repudiation of militarization of the militias was debated inside the Iron Column as it was in every other confederal column. In the end, the Column's assembly gave its approval to militarization, since it would otherwise be denied weapons, pay and provisions. Then again, in the event of its being disbanded, there was a danger that the militians might enlist into other, already militarized units.
2. Frank Mintz *La autogestión en la España revolucionaria* (La Piqueta, Madrid, 1977) pp. 295-308. Also Abel Paz, op. cit. pp. 275-294. And Paul Sharkey *The Friends of Durruti: A Chronology* (Editorial Crisol, Tokyo, May 1984).
3. Jaime Balius, Pablo Ruiz and Francisco Pellicer were the leading organizers behind the meeting held by the Friends of Durruti in the Poliorama Theater on Sunday, April 19, 1937.
4. See Jaime Balius's interview with Pablo Ruiz in the newspaper *La Noche* No. 3545 (March 24, 1937): and *El Amigo del Pueblo* No. 5 (July 21, 1937): and Paul Sharkey, op. cit.
5. "Ponencia que a la Asamblea del Sindicato presenta la sección de periodistas para que sea tomada en consideración y elevada al Pleno y pueda servir de controversia al informe que presente el director interino de *Solidaridad Obrera*," dated Barcelona, February 21 and 22, 1937, on behalf of the Asamblea de la Sección de Periodistas. [Document on deposit with the Archivo Histórico Municipal de Barcelona (AHMB).]
6. See some of the new articles carried by *Solidaridad Obrera*, like "La ciudad de Barcelona" (August 18, 1936), "En el nuevo local del Comite de Milicias Antifascistas" (August 23, 1936), "Ha caido en el cumplimiento de su deber" (October 3, 1936), "Los galeotos de la retaguardia" (October 4, 1936), "Solidaridad con los caidos. . ." (October 9, 1936) or "Los pájaros de la revolución" (October 16, 1936).
See also, in the September and October 1936 editions of *Solidaridad Obrera*, articles similar to those of Balius, under the bylines of Mingo, Floreal Ocaña, Gilabert, etc.
7. Balius's regular column was headlined "Como en la guerra," and, on occasion, the articles were not credited. Endériz, among others, also had a regular column.
8. See some of the articles above Balius's byline carried on the cover, like "No podemos olvidar. 6 de octubre" (October 6, 1936), "la revolución no ha

de frenarse. El léxico de la prensa burguesa es de un sabor contrarevolucionario" (October 15, 1936), "Como en la guerra. En los frentes de combate no han de faltar prendas que son indispensables para sobrellevar la campaña de invierno" (October 16, 1936).

9. We must not omit to highlight (whether or not it was written by Balius) the editorial carried anonymously by *Solidaridad Obrera* (October 11, 1936) under the headline "Ha de constituirse el Consejo Nacional de Defensa," because of the way in which it was taken up later in *El Amigo del Pueblo,* as one of the most original points in the Friends of Durruti's revolutionary program, to wit, the formation of a Revolutionary Junta or National Defense Council.

10. See some of these articles of a political nature, in addition to those named above: "Ha de imponerse un tributo de guerra" (September 8, 1936), "Once de septiembre" (September 11, 1936), "Como en la guerra. Es de inmediata necesidad el racionamiento del consumo" (September 16, 1936), "Han triunfado las tacticas revolucionarias" (September 23, 1936), "Como en la guerra. La justicia ha de ser inflexible" (October 11, 1936), "Seamos conscientes. Por una moral revolucionaria" (October 18, 1936), "Problemas fundamentales de la revolución. La descentralización es la garantia que ha de recabar la clase trabajadora en defensa de la prerrogativas que se debaten en las lineas de fuego" (October 24, 1936), "Como en la guerra. Los agiotistas tienen pena de la vida" [an uncredited article which can be put down to Balius] (October 31, 1936), "Como en la guerra. La justicia ha de ser fulminante e intachable" [attributable to Balius] (November 1, 1936), "Como en la guerra. Se ha de establecer un control riguroso de la población" (November 3, 1936), "La cuestión catalana" (December 2, 1936), "El testamento de Durruti" (December 6, 1936) and "La revolución de julio ha de cellal el paso a los arribislas" (December 17, 1936).

11. See the "Ponencia. . ." on deposit with the AHMB.

12. See the "Ponencia. . ." on deposit with the AHMB.

13. See Balius's remarks on the replacement of Liberto Callejas by Jacinto Toryho as managing editor of *Solidaridad Obrera,* the CNT's leading daily newspaper: "And I who served as editor [of *Soli*] alongside Alejandro Gilabert, Fontaura and others, ought to make it clear that a distinction has to be made between *Soli* under Liberto Callejas's management and the *Soli* run by Jacinto Toryho. As long as Callejas was director the CNT's July gains were at all times defended, and anarchist principles praised and propagated. But once Jacinto Toryho was imposed as director of *Solidaridad Obrera,* by the counter-revolutionaries ensconced in the committees, that is, by the cabal which has no goal other than to dispose of the authentic CNT, then not only was militarization championed, as F. Montseny implies, [but there was] something else. Day after day one could read in *Soli* about comrade Prieto and comrade Negrin.

Let us come out with it all: men of dubious repute, like Canovas Cervantes and Leandro Blanco, former editor of *El Debate*, joined the editorial team at *Soli*. Life at *Soli* became impossible. I quit." (Jaime Balius "Por los fueros de la verdad," in *Le Combat Syndicaliste* of September 2, 1971.)
See also "Ponencia . . ."
14. Radio broadcast reprinted in *Solidaridad Obrera* (November 6,1936). That edition of *Soli* attributed the following words to Durruti: "If this militarization decreed by the Generalidad is intended to frighten us and force iron discipline upon us, they have made a mistake, and we invite those who devised the Decree to go to the front . . . and then we will be able to make comparisons with the morale and discipline of the rearguard. Rest easy. On the front, there is no chaos, no indiscipline."
15. Balius's most outstanding articles carried in *Ideas* are as follows: "La pequera burguesia es impotente para reconstruir España destruida por el fascismo" (No. 1, December 29, 1936), "La Revolución ha de seguir avanzando" (No. 3, January 14, 1937), "El fracaso de la democracia burguesa" (No. 4, January 21, 1937), "La Revolución exige un supremo esfuerzo" (No. 7, February 11, 1937), "Despues del 19 de julio" (No. 14, April 1, 1937) and "Hagamos la revolución" (No. 15, April 8, 1937).
No. 11 of *Ideas* (March 11, 1937) carries an unsigned article entitled "¡Destitución inmediata de Aiguadé!," denouncing the counterrevolutionary activities of the Generalidad's councilor for Security, two months ahead of the May events, over his theft of twelve tanks from the CNT through the use of forged documents, and over his systematic recruitment of monarchist and fascist personnel into the Generalidad's Security Corps.
16. Balius states: "It is intolerable that an individual without the slightest support in the workplace should attempt to lay claim to the Power which belongs to the working people alone. That of itself is enough to tell us that, had he a sizable body of men at his disposal, that same politician would once again place the working class in the capitalist harness. [. . .] For those guilty of the Revolution's failure to sweep aside the enemies of the working class, we have to look to the workers' ranks, to those who, for want of decisiveness in the early stages have allowed the counterrevolutionary forces to grow to such dimensions that it will be an expensive business to put them in their place."
17. Issue No. 1 of *Ideas* carries the following list of the editors of and contributors to the "mouthpiece of the Bajo Llobregat Libertarian Movement": Liberto Callejas (former director of *Solidaridad Obrera*), Evelio G. Fontaura, Floreal Ocaña, José Abella and Ginés Alonso, as editors. And Senén Félix as administrator. As contributors: Jaime Balius, Nieves Núñez, Elias Garcia, Severino Campos, José Peirats (director of *Acracia* in Lerida and future historian of the Spanish anarchist movement), Fraterno Alba, Dr. Amparo Poch, Ricardo

Riccetti, Ramón Calopa, Luzbel Ruiz, Vicente Marcet, Manuel Viñuales, Antonio Ocaña, Tomás and Benjamin Cano Ruiz, Francisco Carreño (a member of the Durruti Column, its delegate to Moscow and a future leading militant of the Friends of Durruti), Antollio Vidal, Felipe Alaiz (a prominent anarchist theorist), Acracio Progreso, Manuel Pérez, José Alberola and Miguel Giménez. The cartoonists included Joaquin Cadena and E. Badia and Bonet.

18. For *Acracia* of Lerida and its director, Peirats, it is interesting to consult the latter's memoirs, especially for the stark description of the tremendous disappointment which the CNT-FAI's collaboration with the government created in lots of anarchist militants. See José Peirats Valls "Memorias," in *Suplementos Anthropos* No. 18, Barcelona, January 1990.

In addition to *Ideas* in Hospilalet and *Acracia* in Lerida, the following were prominent anarcho-syndicalist opposition newspapers critical of the CNT's collaborationism: *Ciudad y Campo* in Tortosa and *Nosotros* in Valencia. Mention should also be made of *Ruta* and *Esfuerzo,* organs of the Libertarian Youth of Catalonia.

19. The notice in *La Noche* (March 2, 1937) states:

> "At the instigation of a number of comrades of the anarchist Buenaventura Durruti who knew how to end his life with those same yearnings for liberation that marked his whole personal trajectory, it has been adjudged appropriate that a group should be launched to keep alive the memory of the man who, by dint of his integrity and courage, was the very symbol of the revolutionary era begun in mid-July. We invite all comrades who cherished Durruti while he was alive and who, after that giant's death, have cherished the memory of that great warrior, to join the "Friends of Durruti."
>
> The "Friends of Durruti" is not just another club. Our intention is that the Spanish Revolution should be filled with our Durruti's revolutionary spirit. The Friends of Durruti remain faithful to the last words uttered by our comrade in the very heart of Barcelona in denunciation of the work of the counterrevolution, tracing, with a manly hand, the route that we must take.
>
> To enroll in our association, you must be a CNT member and furnish evidence of a record of struggle and of love for ideas and for the revolution. For the time being, applications are being received at Rambla de Cataluña, 15, principal, (CNT Journalists' branch) between five and seven in the evening.
>
> — The steering commission

20. Articles in *La Noche* bearing Mingo's signature are "Nuestra labor. La Revolución ha de seguir avallzando" (April 2, 1937), "Al pueblo se le ha de hablar claro"(April 8, 1937), "La Revolución exige una labor depuradora" (April 9, 1937) and "Una labor revolucionaria. La revalorización de los Municipios" (April 13, 1937).
21. Mingo: "Una labor revolucionaria. La revalorización de los Municipios," in *La Noche* (April 13, 1937).
22. The pamphlet [which we have not been able to consult] jointly credited to Jaime Balius and Pablo Ruiz is entitled *Figols, 8 de enero, 8 de diciembre, y Octubre* and was published by Editorial Renacer.
23. Although undated, these pamphlets by Balius came after October 1934 and before July 1936, and in order of publication they were: Jaime Balius *De Jaca a Octubre* Editorial Renacer, [Barcelona] undated; Jaime Balius *Octubre catalan* Editorial Renacer,[Barcelona] undated; and, Jaime Balius *El nacionalisrno y el proletariado* Editorial Renacer, [Barcelona] undated.
24. As Balius stated in his letter of June 1, 1978 to Paul Sharkey: "I belonged to the FAI's Renacer group along with comrades Pablo Ruiz, Francisco Pellicer, since deceased and Bruno Lladó, likewise deceased." [Letter made available by Paul Sharkey, whom we thank for this information.]

5. The Friends of Durruti Group from its Inception up to the May Events

In October 1936, the order militarizing the People's Militias provoked great discontent among the anarchist militians of the Durruti Column on the Aragon front. Following protracted and bitter arguments, in February 1937 around thirty out of the 1,000 volunteer militians based in the Gelsa sector decided to quit the front and return to the rearguard.[1] The agreement was that militians opposed to militarization would be relieved over a fortnight. These then left the front, taking their weapons with them.

Back in Barcelona, along with other anarchists (advocates of prosecuting and pursuing the July revolution, and opposed to the CNT's collaboration with the government), the militians from Gelsa decided to form an affinity group, like the many other affinity groups[2] in existence in anarcho-syndicalist circles. And so, the Group was formally launched in March 1937,[3] following a lengthy period of incubation that had lasted for several months, beginning in October 1936. The Steering Committee made the decision to adopt the name "Friends of Durruti Group," the name being, in part, an invocation of their common origins as former militians in the Durruti Column, and, as Balius was correct in saying, there was no reference intended to Durruti's thinking, but rather to his heroic death and mythic status in the eyes of the populace.

The Group's central headquarters was located in the Ramblas, at the junction with the Calle Hospital. The membership of the Group grew remarkably quickly. Somewhere between four thousand and five thousand Group membership cards were issued. One of the essential requirements for Group membership was CNT membership. The growth of the Group was a consequence of anarchist unease with the CNT's policy of compromise.

The Group was frenetically active and dynamic. Between its formal launch on March 17 and May 3, the Group mounted a number of rallies (in the Poliorama Theater on April 19 and the Goya Theater on May 2), issued several manifestoes and handbills and covered the walls of Barcelona with posters setting out its program.[4] Two points stood out in that program: 1. All power to the working class; and, 2. Democratic workers', peasants' and combatants' organs as the expression of this workers' power,[5] which was encapsulated in the term Revolutionary Junta.

They also called for the trade unions to take over the economic and political governance of the country completely. And when they talked about trade unions, they meant the CNT unions, not the UGT unions. In fact, some of the members of the Group had quit the UGT in order to affiliate straight away to the CNT, thereby fulfilling the essential prerequisite for membership of the Friends of Durruti.

In reality, although the working class provenance of the Group's members ensured that they were CNT members, most were members of the FAI, on which basis it can be stated that the Friends of Durruti Group was a group of anarchists which took a stand on purist anarchist doctrine and opposed the collaborationist State-centered policy of the leadership of the CNT and of the FAI proper.

They had the upper hand inside the Foodstuffs Union, which had ramifications all over Catalonia, as well as in the mining areas of Sallent, Suria, Figols, and Cardona, in the Upper Llobregat comarca. They were influential in other unions too, where they were in the minority. Some members belonged to the Control Patrols. But at no time did they constitute a fraction or group, nor did they attempt to infiltrate the Patrols.

We cannot characterize the Group as a comprehensively conscious, organized group that would undertake methodical activity. It was one of many more or less informal anarchist groups formed around certain characteristic affinities. Nor were they good propagandists or theorists, but instead a group of proletarians alive to an **instinctive** need to confront the CNT's policy of appeasement and the accelerating process of counterrevolution.

Without question, their most outstanding spokesmen were Jaime Balius and Pablo Ruiz. From March 1937 to May 1937, the Libertarian Youth of Catalonia[6] also set out in their wall newspaper[7] demands similar to those of the Friends of Durruti.

On April 14, 1937, the Group issued a Manifesto[8] in which it set its face against the bourgeois commemoration of the anniversary of the proclamation of the Republic, on the grounds that it was merely a pretext for reinforcing bourgeois institutions and the counterrevolution. Instead of commemoration of the Republic and in opposition to the Generalidad and Luis Companys, which were the cutting edge of bourgeois counterrevolution, the Friends of Durruti proposed commemoration of July 19th and exhorted the CNT and the FAI to come up with a revolutionary escape route from the dead-end street of the Generalidad government's crisis. That crisis started on March 4th with a decree ordering dissolution of the Control Patrols: the CNT's failure to comply implied the exclusion of CNT personnel from the Generalidad government.

The Manifesto catalogued a host of trespasses against revolutionaries, from the most celebrated case of Maroto, which even drew indignant comment from the docile *Solidaridad Obrera,* through to lesser known cases, such as the incidents in Olesa de Montserrat. In fact, the Manifesto reiterated the program points which had been incubating since early March in articles by Balius, Mingo and others in *La Noche.* And these were summed up in the opening paragraph of the Manifesto:

> The capitalist State, which suffered a formidable setback in the memorable events of July, is still extant, thanks to the counterrevolutionary endeavor of the petit-bourgeoisie [. . .]
>
> The Generalidad crisis is categorical evidence that we have to build a new world, wholly dispensing with statist formulas.
>
> It is high time that the legion of petit-bourgeois, shopkeepers and guards was ruthlessly swept aside. There can be no compromise with counterrevolution. [. . .]
>
> This is a time of life or death for the working class. [. . .] Let us not hesitate.
>
> The CNT and the FAI, being the organizations that reflect the people's concerns, must come up with a revolutionary way out of the dead-end street [. . .] We have the organs that must supplant a State in ruins. The Trade Unions and Municipalities must take charge of economic and social life [. . .]"

On Sunday April 18, 1937, the Group held a rally in the Poliorama Theater, by way of bringing its existence and its program to the attention of the public.[9] Jaime Balius, Pablo Ruiz (delegate from the Gelsa Group), Francisco Pellicer (a delegate from the Iron Column) and Francisco Carreño (a member of the Durruti Column's War Committee) all spoke. The meeting was a great success and the ideas set out by the speakers were roundly applauded.

On the first Sunday in May 1937 (May 2) the Group held a further introductory rally at the Goya Theater: the theater was filled to overflowing and the rally moved those attending to delirious enthusiasm. A documentary film entitled "Nineteenth of July" was screened, reliving the most emotive passages from the revolutionary events of July 19, 1936. The speakers were De Pablo [Could this be Pablo Ruiz?], Jaime Balius, Liberto Callejas and Francisco Carreño. The meeting heard a prediction that an attack upon the workers by the reactionaries was now imminent.

The leadership committees of the CNT and the FAI did not pay undue heed to this new opposition emanating from within the libertarian movement, despite the scathing criticisms directed at themselves. In anarchist circles it was not unusual for groups to bubble to the surface, enjoying a meteoric rise, only to vanish into nothing as quickly as they had arisen.

The program spelled out by the Friends of Durruti **prior to May 1937** was characterized by its emphasis upon trade union management of the economy, upon criticism of all the parties and their statist collaborationism, as well as a certain reversion to anarchist doctrinal purity.

The Friends of Durruti set out their program in the poster with which they covered the walls of Barcelona towards the end of April 1937. Those posters which, even then, **ahead of the events of May**, argued the need to **replace** the bourgeois Generalidad government of Catalonia with a Revolutionary Junta, stated as follows:[10]

> Friends of Durruti Group. To the working class:
> 1. Immediate establishment of a Revolutionary Junta made up of workers of city and countryside and of combatants.
> 2. Family wage. Ration cards. Trade union direction of the economy and supervision of distribution.
> 3. Liquidation of the counterrevolution.
> 4. Creation of a revolutionary army.
> 5. Absolute working class control of public order.
> 6. Steadfast opposition to any armistice.
> 7. Proletarian justice.
> 8. Abolition of personnel changes.
>
> Attention, workers: our group is opposed to the continued advance of the counterrevolution. The public order decrees sponsored by Aiguadé are not to be heeded. We insist upon the release of Maroto and other comrades detained.
>
> All power to the working class. All economic power to the unions.
>
> Rather than the Generalidad, a Revolutionary Junta!

The April 1937 poster foreshadowed and explains the leaflet issued during the events in May and incorporates many of the themes and concerns dealt with by Balius in the articles he published in *Solidaridad Obrera*, *La Noche* and *Ideas* (especially revolutionary justice, prisoner exchanges, the need for the rearguard to take the war to heart, etc.). For the first time the need was posited for a Revolutionary Junta to supplant the bourgeois Generalidad government. This Revolutionary Junta[11] was defined as a revolutionary government comprised of workers, peasants and militians.

Most significant of all is the consolidated message of the last three slogans. Replacement of the bourgeois Generalidad government by a Revolutionary Junta appears alongside the watchwords "All power to the working class" and "All economic power to the unions."[12]

The political program implicit in this poster immediately before the events of May is undoubtedly the most advanced and lucid offered by any of the existing proletarian groups, and makes of the Friends of Durruti Group a **revolutionary vanguard of the proletariat** of Spain at this critical and crucial juncture as the POUM and the Bolshevik-Leninist Section of Spain were to acknowledge.[13]

Notes for Chapter 5

1. We can find a detailed description of the Gelsa militians and their opposition to militarization, which was closely connected with the launch of the Friends of Durruti, in the interview with Pablo Ruiz in *La Noche* Año XIV, No. 3545, of March 24, 1937.
See also the claims made by Balius himself: "The Friends of Durruti Group has its origins in the opposition to militarization. It was the Gelsa Militians Group that relocated en masse to Barcelona. At the head of the Gelsa Group was comrade Eduardo Cervero. So, in the Catalan rearguard, there was a considerable number of comrades from the Aragon front around, sharing the opinion that there was no way that the libertarian spirit of the militias could be abjured. Lest we embark upon an interminable list of comrades who moved to the Catalan capital with arms and baggage, allow me to recall, with great affection, Progreso Ródenas, Pablo Ruiz, Marcelino Benedicto and others. It was agreed that a group should be set up in Barcelona, and it was determined that it would be under the aegis of the symbol of Buenaventura Durruti. Other members of the Durruti Group included comrades Alejandro Gilabert, Francisco Carreño, Máximo Franco, the delegate from the Rojinegra Division, Ponzán, Santana Calero, and lots of others." (Jaime Balius "Por los fueros de la verdad" in *Le Combat syndicaliste* of September 2, 1971).

With regard to the number of militians from the Gelsa Group who, having repudiated militarization, decided to quit the front, taking their weapons with them, Pablo Ruiz is a lot more statistically precise, and probably a lot nearer the mark. "[After taking part in the storming of the Atarazanas barracks], I joined the Durruti Column, and I led the 4th Gelsa Group, comprising over a thousand militians (. . .) whenever the Popular Army was foisted upon us from within (. . .) I resigned and rejoined the rearguard along with three decades of comrades. On that basis and at the instigation of comrade Balius, we founded the Friends of Durruti Group (. . .)" [Pablo Ruiz "Elogio póstumo de Jaime Balius" in *Le Combat Syndicaliste/Solidaridad Obrera* of January 22, 1981]
2. The FAI was organized as a federation of affinity groups. During the civil war, prominence was achieved by affinity groups like "Nosotros" (which had previously gone under the name "Los Solidarios"), "Nervio," "A," "Z," "Los de Ayer y Los de Hoy," "Faro," etc.
3. The newspaper *La Noche* on March 2, 1937 (page 6) carried the first report on the foundation of the Group, which was formally launched on March 17, 1937, according to this notice in the March 18,1937 edition of *La Noche*:

> The 'Friends of Durruti' Group has been launched. A steering committee appointed. The meeting to launch the 'Friends of Durruti' was held last night.
>
> The social premises — located on the first floor of 1, Ramblas de las Flores — were packed with people. Proceedings got underway on the stroke of ten o'clock. A panel was appointed to oversee the discussions. Several comrades from the front and from the rearguard took part in the discussion. Every one of the comrades who spoke reaffirmed his absolute support for the postulates of the CNT and FAI. There was broad discussion of the revolutionary course followed since July 19 and it was palpable that all of the assembled comrades wish the Revolution to press ahead. Certain counterrevolutionary maneuvers were lashed severely. [. . .]
>
> In a disembodied way, our Durruti presided over the launch of the group. It was notable that there was no hint of idolatry, but rather a desire to carry out the wishes of our ill-fated comrade.
>
> Next, the steering committee was appointed, along with a working party to draft the intentions by which the new group is to be informed. [. . .] The steering committee is made up as follows: secretary, Felix Martinez: vice-secretary, Jaime Balius: treasurer, José Paniagua: book-keeper, Antonio Puig Garreta: committee

members, Francisco Carreño, Pablo Ruiz, Antonio Romero, Serafin Sobias, Eduardo Cervero. The working part comprises: Pablo Ruiz, J. Marin, Jaime Balius, Francisco Carreño and José Esplugas.

Before the proceedings were wound up, the gathering agreed by acclamation that a telegram should be sent to the CNT National Committee, demanding the release of comrade Maroto and of the comrades incarcerated in Valencia.

4. Let us attempt to catalog all of the manifestoes, handbills, notices and posters signed by the Friends of Durruti Group, insofar as we know them. We shall not indicate place of publication because that is the city of Barcelona throughout. Virtually all of these documents can be found in the Archivo Historico Municipal de Barcelona (AHMB):

1. "Al pueblo trabajador" [*Manifesto* issued late March 1937. Double-sided handbill.]
2. "Al pueblo trabajador" [*Manifesto* opposing the commemoration of the anniversary of April 14.]
3. '"¡Trabahadiers! Acudid el próximo dimingo, dia 18, al MITIN que la Agrupación Los Amigos de Durruti celebralá en el Teatro Poliorama" [*Notice* advertising the rally on April 18, 1937.]
4. "Agrupación de Los Amigos de Durruti. A la clase trabajadora." [*Poster* pasted on walls and trees. Late April 1937.]
5. "ACTO organizado por la Agrupación Los Amigos de Durruti. Domingo, 2 de mayo a las 10 de la mañana, en el TEATRO GOYA." [*Notice* of the May 2, 1937 rally.]
6. "CNT-FAI. Agrupación 'Los Amigos de Durruti'. ¡TRABAJADORES!" [*Handbill* distributed on the barricades on May 5, 1937.]
7. "CNT-FAI. Agrupacion 'Los Amigos de Durruti'. Trabajadores." [*Manifesto* distributed on May 8, 1937.]
8. "Trabajadores. Miércoles dia 19. Aparecerá el 'Los Amigos de Durruti'." [Notice of the appearance of the first issue of *El Amigo del Pueblo,* scheduled for May 19, 1937.]

There are also some notices of lectures by Francisco Pellicer, sponsored by the CNT Foodstuffs Union, which we have not included.

5. See Juan Andrade "CNT-POUM" in *La Batalla* of May 1, 1937. Reprinted in Juan Andrade *La revolución espanola dia a dia* (Ed. Nueva Era, Barcelona, 1979, p. 248.) The extract in which Andrade refers to the Friends of Durruti is this one:

For instance, the 'Friends of Durruti' have framed their program points in posters in every street in Barcelona. We are absolutely in agreement with the watchwords that the 'Friends of Durruti' have issued with regard to the current situation. This is a program we accept, and on the basis of which we are ready to come to whatever agreements they may put to us. There are two items in those watchwords which are also fundamental for us. All Power to the working class and democratic organs of the workers, peasants and combatants, as the expression of proletarian Power.

6. *Ruta*, the mouthpiece of the Libertarian Youth of Catalonia, had been radically opposed to the CNT's collaborationism since November 1936. Between March 1937 and late May 1937, it carried articles by Santana Calero (a member of the Libertarian Youth of Malaga), who was also a prominent contributor to *El Amigo del Pueblo* and a member of the Friends of Durruti. Issue No. 25 of *Ruta*, dated April 1, 1937, carried an article from the Friends of Durruti Group, entitled "Por el concepto anarquista de la revolución," in which the same arguments are set out as in the late March handbill/manifesto: that the CNT-FAI had failed to impose itself on July 19 and agreed to collaborate as a minority player and afforded full scope to the petit-bourgeoisie: that the war and the revolution had to be one: "the war and the revolution are two aspects that cannot be dissevered. The War is the defense of the revolution": that the unions should have the direction of the economy: that the army and public order should be under workers' control: that arms had to be in the hands of workers only, by way of a guarantee of the revolution: that the petite bourgeoisie should man the fortifications battalions: that the rearguard should take the war to heart: that work should be compulsory and unionization obligatory, etc.
7. This was *Esfuerzo: Periódico mural de las Juventudes Libertarias de Cataluña.* A weekly publication, comprising of one poster-sized page for posting on walls, it came out between the second week of March and the second week of May. Completely anonymous, it was made up, not of articles, but of watchwords, short manifestoes and appeals. It was a highly original wall newspaper. The following "articles" stand out: "El dilema: Fascismo o Revolución social" (in No. 1, second week of March 1937), "Consignas de la Juventud Revolucionaria" (No. 2, third week of March), "El Orden Público tiene su garantia en las Patrullas de Control..." (No. 3, fourth week of March), "Los 'affaires' por la substracción de 11 tanques. La provocación de Orden Publico en Reus, por Rodriguez Salas . . ." and "A los ochos meses de revolución" (No. 4, first week of April 1937). The last issue of this wall newspaper, No. 9, is dated the second week of May 1937. Although the Friends of Durruti Group is never mentioned by name, its watchwords, vision and ideological content

were very similar to those articulated and championed by the Friends of Durruti.

8. 'Friends of Durruti' Group "Al pueblo trabajador" Barcelona [April 14, 1937]

9. This meeting to introduce the Group was reported in detail by Rosalio Negrete and Hugo Oehler in a report written and date-lined in Barcelona the same day. That report was first published in *Fourth International* Volume 2, No. 12, (1937). See *Revolutionary History* Volume 1, No. 2, (1988), London, pp. 34-35.

The meeting had been called by means of handbills announcing that Francisco Pellicer would speak on the problelm of subsistence, Pablo Ruiz on the revolutionary army, Jaime Balius on the war and the revolution, Francisco Carreño on trade union unity and political collaboration, and V. Perez Combina on public order and the present time.

The following notice was carried in the daily newspaper *La Noche* (19 April 1937) about the progress of the meeting:

> Yesterday morning, in the Poliorama Theatre, a meeting was held by the Friends of Durruti Group. There was a considerable attendance and the meeting was chaired by comrade Romero, who, after a few short remarks outlining the meaning of the meeting, called upon Francisco Pellicer, who opened with a recollection of Durruti.
>
> Next, attention turned to the problem of subsistence, and he stated that it was impossible to eat on current rates of pay [. . .] Pablo Ruiz spoke on the revolutionary army [. . .] Then Jaime Balius read some jottings [. . .] in which he reviewed the initial fighting against fascism on July 19 [. . .] He stated that the Revolution should go hand in hand with the war and that both have to be won. [. . .] Francisco Carreño spoke last on the topic 'trade union unity and political collaboration' [. . .] He, like the rest of the speakers, was very warmly applauded.

10. *Acta de la sessió consistorial del 22-5-1937 del Ajuntamente de Sabadell*, Archivo Histórico de Sabadell. On page 399 of the book of minutes No. 16, the poster from the Friends of Durruti, issued in April 1937, is reproduced in full. This poster, which council member Bruno Lladó (who was also the comarcal delegate of the Generalidad's department of economy [headed by Diego Abad de Santillán]) had put up in his office on Sunday, May 2nd, joined the book of evidence against him when the councilor was accused of inciting rebellion against the Generalidad government in the course of the events of May in Barcelona. The text of this poster, according to the minutes of the May 22, 1937 sitting of Sabadell Council was reprinted in Andreu Castells: *Sabadell, informe de*

l'oposició. Annex per a la história de Sabadell (Vol. V) Guerra i revolucio (1936-1939) (Ed. Riutort, Sabadell, 1982, p. 22.8)

11. The definition of the Revolutionary Junta offered by the Friends of Durruti was not always the same, as we shall see anon. But the significance of the watchwords in the April poster eluded no one. Establishment of a Revolutionary Junta implied not only the winding up of the bourgeois Generalidad government, but the introduction of dictatorship of the proletariat: "all power to the working class" and "all economic power to the unions." In an interview granted to *Lutte Ouvriere* in 1939, Munis took the line that the terms "revolutionary junta" and "soviets," as used by the Friends of Durruti, were synonymous.

12. Balius was very conscious of the importance of the watchwords set out in the April 1937 poster. "May 1 1937 is the Spanish Kronstadt. In Catalonia, uprising was feasible only by virtue of the CNT's might. And just as, in Russia, the sailors and workers of Kronstadt arose to a cry of "All power to the soviets," so the Friends of Durruti Group called for "All power to the unions," and we did so publicly in the many posters stuck up all over the city of Barcelona and in the manifesto we issued and managed to print up while the battle raged." (Jaime Balius "Por los fueros de la verdad" in *Le combat Syndicaliste* of September 2, 1971)

See also Munis's comments in *La Voz Leninista* No. 2 of August 23, 1937.

13. Juan Andrade "CNT-POUM" in *La Batalla* of May 1, 1937. See also G. Munis "La Junta Revolucionaria y los 'Amigos de Durruti"' in *La Voz Leninista* No. 2, of August 23, 1937.

EL AMIGO DEL PUEBLO

PORTAVOZ DE LOS AMIGOS DE DURRUTI

Año I.—Núm. 4.—20 Cts. Martes, 22 Junio de 1937

La barricada

por ELEUTERIO ROIG

Tras informe y heterogéneo montón,
hombres duros y enfebrecidos,
empuñan el fusil, oprimido el corazón,
bajo una lluvia de plomo,
y entre el dolor lacerante de agónicos gemidos.
Es la barricada...
Recio yunque do se forja la vindicta.
Muro regolante que brazos viriles levantaron,
inflamado el pecho,
al grito candente de rebeldía.

En su parte alta,
ondea al viento,
cimbor y amenazante,
sanguinolento
trapo rojo, que fué percala de un caído;
ahora es baluarte invencible y bravío,
que simboliza la revuelta,
y es bandera de combate.
Tiembla el verdugo al contemplarla,
y a sus pies se doblega y se abate.
Clava el plomo en su frente,
y el esbirro en él se estrella.
¡No pasan!
La chusma cruel
rola del sagrario y la tiara.
Las fuerzas conjugadas
del opresión y la ignominia,
también se estrellan.
¡No pasan...!
Y ante el muro se doblegan
impotentes y vencidas.
Simboliza un mundo nuevo,
contra otro carcomido.
La verdad, ante la mentira.
Lo humano, frente a lo divino.
¡Ciclópeo muro de justicia
que jamás será abatido!
¡Protesta violenta contra tiranos y tiranos!
¡Muro informe de iras contenidas
en las falanges [illegible]!
¡Terror de los malvados!
¡Muro terrible; [illegible]
[illegible] de soberbias!

* * *

Sus piedras [illegible] de la calle—,
y de las casas, el mueblaje...
los objetos todos que la forman y dan vida,
están bañados en sangre.
La turba de asesinos y cobardes,
provocaron la tragedia en su malvada arremetida
Mas no cede.
Altanera y heroica,
el fin espera de la lucha.
Tras ella se guarece
un puñado de hombres bravos,
que jalonan la victoria.
Lo sabe. Por eso los oculta.
Por eso los protege.
Son hombres del pueblo. Hombres tenaces
que ante el amo no se doblan.
No temen a la muerte.
El polvo de la derrota,
no morderán porque esgrimen la razón...
y eso les alienta y fortalece.
Corre impetuosa por sus venas,
volcánica sangre de rebeldes.
Baluarte de corrientes
contra un mundo de infamia.
Mundo podrido.
Viejo mundo de opresión y de ignorancia.

* * *

Una nube espesa y agria,
envuelve del muro, la trágica silueta.
Olor a pólvora y a sangre paria,
despide aquel informe, heterogéneo, montón
[de cosas.
Dejando exhibir la calzada,
la herida dolorosa de su vientre.
Impávida se yergue
su silueta redentora.
Es un faro de esperanza.
Templo de justicia.
Crisol de rebeldía... "
... ...
Es la barricada.

Lo mismo que el 19 de Julio los trabajadores de Barcelona se rebelaron contra el fascismo negro, el 9 de Mayo lo hicieron contra las conjuraciones e intrigas de los partidos pequeño-burgueses aliados con el capitalismo internacional

Nosotros, 'agentes provocadores e irresponsables,' propugnamos:

Dirección de la vida económica y social por los Sindicatos.

Municipio Libre.

El ejército y el orden público ha de estar controlados por la clase trabajadora. Disolución de los Cuerpos Armados. Mantenimiento de los Comités de Defensa y de las Consejerías de Defensa.

Las armas han de estar en poder del proletariado. Los fusiles son la garantía máxima de las conquistas revolucionarias. Nadie más que la clase trabajadora puede disponer de ellas.

Abolición de las jerarquías. Batallones de fortificación integrados por los enemigos del proletariado.

Sindicación forzosa. Bolsa de Trabajo. Cese de recomendaciones para conseguir trabajo. Carta de racionamiento. Trabajo obligatorio. En la retaguardia se ha de vivir para la guerra.

Socialización de todos los medios de producción y cambio. Lucha a muerte contra el fascismo y sus encubridores. Depuración de la retaguardia. Creación de los Comités de vecinos.

Implantación inmediata del salario familiar sin excepciones burocráticas. La Guerra y la revolución ha de alcanzar a todos por igual. Supresión del Parlamento burgués. Suspensión de pasaportes.

Movilización frente a la contrarrevolución.

Desobediencia total a las medidas coactivas del Estado: tales como la aplicación de la censura, desarme de los trabajadores, incautación de las emisoras de radio por el Estado, etc.

Oposición decidida a que los medios de producción sean Municipalizados, mientras la clase trabajadora no sea dueña absoluta del país.

Retorno al sentido ampliamente revolucionario de nuestras organizaciones.

Oposición total a la colaboración gubernamental por ser totalmente contraproducente para la emancipación del proletariado.

Guerra a muerte a los especuladores, a los burócratas, a los causantes del alza de las subsistencias.

En pie de guerra contra todo armisticio.

Lágrimas de mujer

No podemos borrar de nuestra mente aquellos días venturosos en que el proletariado se batía en la calle. Aun continúa prendido en nuestra imaginación el recuerdo glorioso de unas jornadas que marcan un jalón esplendoroso en los anales del proletariado catalán.

De aquellas fechas iniciales de mayo no podemos alejar una sensación altamente sentida. Una escena de un hondo patetismo nos conmovió hondamente. Nos sentimos torpes para transcribirla con la pluma, pero el dolor que aún despedaza nuestras entrañas nos impulsa a rasgar un silencio que se había cobijado en nuestras propias carnes.

Nos acordamos con tal precisión de las escenas vividas que nos resistimos a creer que haya transcurrido una hilera de fechas. El tableteo de las ametralladoras, el crepitar de los fusiles y las detonaciones contundentes de las bombas persiste en los pliegues del aparato auditivo. Fué en mayo que percibimos tales sensaciones. No obstante, nos hallamos alejados de aquella lucha en la que cayeron por toda una eternidad un gran número de camaradas que los llevaremos mientras vivamos.

El fuego arreciaba. La Rambla había perdido su fisonomía habitual. Las balas cruzaban inquietas. Nuestros enemigos dibujaban las siluetas de los bravos camaradas. Desde las barricadas se abría un fuego intenso contra el adversario que no asomaba el rostro. Los viandantes se habían esfumado.

De pronto, en el fragor del combate aparece una mujer. En su diestra guarda avariciosamente una bomba. Es una mujer entrada en años. Habla. Gesticula. Increpa a unos enemigos que no dan la cara. Llora. Llora a lágrima viva. Esta mujer del pueblo acusa. Denuncia su [illegible] de la furia de las balas que le han matado a su compañero, a un hijo y a su [illegible]. [illegible] por los sollozos. Suplica que la maten. Se acerca a los lugares de peligro. Desea la muerte.

Nos acercamos a ella. Le indicamos que corría un peligro evidente. No conseguimos que abandonase el arroyo. Quería morir. Sus allegados, asesinados por el enemigo, pudieron más que todas nuestras recomendaciones. Era tal el dolor que se había clavado en el corazón de aquella valerosa mujer que ni las balas ni el peligro inminente hacían mella en su cuerpo femenino.

Las lágrimas surcaban sus mejillas. Sus increpaciones trepaban hasta el firmamento preñado de destellos de sangre y de fuego. Sus voces conmovían a la Barcelona rebelde, y daban un colorido de patetismo a la anchurosa vía que acostumbra a albergar a los paseantes que pisan el pavimento de la Rambla en busca de unas [illegible] o de unas caricias amorosas.

La resistencia física de aquella mujer tuvo un límite. Aquel esfuerzo sobrehumano se quebró y como si hubiese sido alcanzada por la ráfaga que en aquel instante asaltaba nuestras efigies, cayó desplomada a los pies del bordillo. En brazos de los galeotes de la revolución fué llevada a una farmacia cercana en donde recobró el conocimiento que la algidez del dolor le había arrebatado.

Hemos vivido instantes de suprema emoción. Hemos visto caer a nuestro lado a muchos camaradas con la vista clavada en el horizonte de la Cataluña proletaria, pero nunca sentimos correr por nuestro cuerpo un escalofrío tan denso, como en el caso de la mujer que desafiaba la muerte porque horas antes le habían arrebatado para siempre a sus seres más queridos.

¡Oh, Mayo glorioso! En aquellos días de lucha se han escrito, con lágrimas y con sangre humana, unas páginas de tamaña brillantez que jamás se borrarán por más que el espacio y la continuidad de los sucesos se interpongan. No olvidaremos. No. No podemos ni queremos.

Cuando la duda nos aqueje, cuando el desfallecimiento se cebe en nuestro ser recordemos aquella mujer, que a pesar de su condición de mujer, desafiaba las balas y amenazaba a los [illegible] que parapetados en las azoteas, y en los campanarios de las Iglesias, lanzaban el plomo en las carnes de los trabajadores.

Recordad a esta mujer. Sus lágrimas eran su derroche de valentía. Y sus gestos la consagraron como heroína de la revolución social. No seamos menos que esta heroína.

Venerable mujer: Quienes estuvimos en la calle contigo permanecemos fieles al espíritu de las jornadas que han ensombrecido tu vida. No olvidamos. Tus lágrimas interpretaron todo un momento. Lloraste por todas las madres, por todas las compañeras y por todos los familiares que como tú se encontraban en el mismo trance. Y tus amenazas las hacemos nuestras.

Una mujer nos da el ejemplo. Como en mayo seguiremos al pie de la barricada.

No entreguéis las armas, camaradas, que ellas son la garantía de la revolución

Exigimos la libertad inmediata de todos los obreros y luchadores presos

6. The May Events[1]

On Saturday, May 1, 1937, there was no May Day demonstration in Barcelona. The Generalidad had announced that this was a day to be worked for the sake of war production, although the real reason was fear of a confrontation between the different labor organizations following heightened tension in several comarcas and localities around Catalonia. That Saturday too the Generalidad council met to look into the worrying public order situation in Catalonia. The council endorsed the effectiveness displayed over the previous few weeks by its councilors for internal security and defense, agreeing to pass a vote of confidence in their ability to resolve **outstanding**[2] public order business.

As the council meeting concluded, there was a meeting of a panel made up of the councilors for defense[3] and internal security and the premier, for the purpose of looking into public order issues.[4] It seems hard to believe that the initiative to seize the Telephone Exchange could have been a personal decision by the councilor for security, Artemi Aiguadé. It is more likely that the decision would have been made by the panel which met after the council meeting on May 1st,[5] or resulted from the incident on Sunday May 2nd, when a telephone conversation between Companys and Azaña (who happened to be in Barcelona) was crassly interrupted by CNT militants. Of course, if the operation failed, the security councilor would carry the full political responsibility. By a stroke of luck, on Monday May 3rd, Companys happened to be on a visit to Benicarló for a meeting with Largo Caballero, conveniently enabling him to dissociate himself from the initial incidents. Be that as it may, Companys' political action, with his blinkered, incomprehensible refusal to dismiss Artemio Aiguadé and Rodriguez Salas,[6] as the CNT had insisted right from May 3rd, was one of the most significant triggers of the armed clashes in the ensuing days.

On Monday May 3, 1937, three truck loads of heavily armed Assault Guards, drew up outside the Telephone Exchange in the Plaza de Cataluña. They were led by Rodriguez Salas, UGT militant and dyed-in-the-wool Stalinist, the officer commanding the public order commissariat in Barcelona. Ever since July 19, the Exchange had been commandeered by the CNT. The sore point was control of telephone links, border controls and the control patrols: since January, the Generalidad republican government and the masses of the CNT had clashed several times over these. It was an inevitable struggle between the republican state apparatus, which was insisting upon complete recovery of all of "its" proper prerogatives, and the CNT membership's defense of the "gains" of July 19, 1936.

Rodriguez Salas attempted to take control of the Telephone Exchange. The CNT militants on the lower floors, caught by surprise, let themselves be disarmed: but on the upper floors dogged resistance was organized, thanks to a machine-gun strategically positioned on the top floor. The news spread like wildfire. Barricades were thrown up immediately all over the city. We can speak of a spontaneous backlash from the Barcelona working class, if we regard as such the initiative shown by the middle ranking cadres of the CNT,[7] as well as the fact that there already existed significant militant organization among the CNT rank and file, in the shape of the district defense committees and the control patrols.[8] Similarly, we can speak of a spontaneous backlash, if we bear it in mind that at no time did an order go out from the CNT leadership, or from the leadership of any other party, before mobilization occurred and barricades were thrown up all around the city.

Nor had anyone issued the call for a general strike, which was the product of class instinct. This was ground ripe for the action that offered itself to the Friends of Durruti. They managed to attend immediately to what the circumstances required. Whilst the workers fought with weapons in hand, they strove to lead them and provide them with a revolutionary objective. But they soon discovered their limitations. They criticized the CNT's leaders, whom they labeled traitors in their May 8 Manifesto, but they were unable to overrule the order to quit the barricades. Nor did they consider supplanting the CNT leadership. They did nothing to see to it that their slogan about establishing a Revolutionary Junta was implemented. They knew that their criticisms of the anarcho-syndicalist leadership would not be enough to wrest control of the CNT organization from it.

C.N.T. **F.A.I.**

Agrupación "Los amigos de Durruti"

¡TRABAJADORES..!

Una Junta revolucionaria. - Fusilamiento de los culpables.
Desarme de todos los Cuerpos armados.
Socialización de la economia.
Disolución de los Partidos políticos que hayan agredido a la clase trabajadora.
No cedamos la calle. La revolución ante todo.
Saludamos a nuestros Camaradas del P.O.U.M. que han confraternizado en la calle con nosotros.

VIVA LA REVOLUCIÓN SOCIAL... ¡ABAJO LA CONTRAREVOLUCIÓN!

On the other hand, the Group was newborn, lacking experience and lacking in prestige with the CNT masses. Its ideas had not managed to permeate the rank and file membership thoroughly.

Wallowing in this situation of powerlessness, they received a note from the POUM Executive Committee, requesting an authorized delegation from the Group to meet them.[9] Jaime Balius, Pablo Ruiz, Eleuterio Roig and Martin were selected.[10] At 7:00 P.M. on May 4 they met in the Principal Palace in the Ramblas with Gorkin, Nin and Andrade.[11] Jointly, they scrutinized the situation, and reached the **unanimous** conclusion that, in view of the CNT[12] and FAI leaderships' opposition to a revolutionary uprising, it was doomed to failure.[13] It was agreed that an orderly withdrawal of the combatants was required, and that the latter should hold on to their weapons.[14] And that this withdrawal should take place once the opposing forces had abandoned their positions. And that assurances were needed that there would be no crack-down on the fighters on the barricades. The next day, the top leaders and officers of the CNT made a further radio broadcast, calling for the fighting to cease. By now the grassroots militants had stopped joking about the "firefighters" of the CNT-FAI and about the Guards kissing Garcia Oliver.

On Wednesday May 5, the Friends of Durruti distributed around the barricades the celebrated handbill that made them famous: it read as follows:

> **CNT-FAI. "Friends of Durruti" Group:** Workers! A Revolutionary Junta. Shoot the culprits. Disarm the armed corps.

> Socialize the economy. Disband the political parties which have turned on the working class. We must not surrender the streets. The revolution before all else. We salute our comrades from the POUM who fraternized with us on the streets. Long live the Social Revolution! Down with the counterrevolution!

This handbill was printed at gun-point on the night of May 4-5, 1937, in a print shop in the Barrio Chino.[15] The improvisation and the Group's lack of infrastructure were obvious. The text had been drafted after that meeting with the POUM Executive Committee at 7:00 P.M. on May 4, by which time the Group and the POUM had agreed upon a defensive withdrawal with no surrender of weapons, and insisting upon assurances that there would be no repression. The handbill, endorsed by the POUM, and reprinted in issue No. 235 of *La Batalla* (on May 6) was not backed by any plan of action and was merely a statement of intent and an appeal to the CNT masses' spontaneity to press ahead with their activities against the encroachments of the counterrevolution. In point of fact, everything hinged upon the decision that the CNT leadership would make. It was absurd and laughable to believe that the CNT masses, in spite of their initial inhibitions, or criticisms, would not follow the leaders of July 19. Only if the CNT leadership were to be supplanted by a revolutionary leadership was there any chance, albeit very slim chance, of the masses' abiding by the revolutionary watchwords and plan of action of a new leadership. But neither the Group nor the POUM made any attempt to unseat the CNT leadership: nor had they drawn up any plan of action. In practice, both pursued a policy of compliance with the CNT leadership's decisions. The POUM's Executive Committee rejected José Rebull's plan to capture the Generalidad and the buildings still holding out in the city center, on the grounds that this was a political matter, not a military one.[16]

Also on May 5 there was a meeting between the POUM Local Committee in Barcelona and the Friends of Durruti — a meeting which the POUMists described as negative,[17] because:

> They [The Friends of Durruti] are unwilling to work directly upon CNT ranks to unseat the leadership, wishing only to influence the movement, with no more responsibility than that.

In the handbill they issued on May 5, the Friends of Durruti suggested concerned action with the POUM. As their immediate objective and to direct the revolution, they proposed that a Revolutionary Junta be established. **But once that watchword had gone out, they did nothing to put it into effect.** They were barricade fighters, rather than organizers.

The suggestion of concerted CNT-FAI-POUM action was nothing more than a salute to the militants from other organizations who had fought alongside them on the barricades. The printed word of the handbill never progressed as far as a hard and fast agreement. They did virtually nothing to unseat the CNT leadership and wrest away control of the CNT masses which repeatedly turned a deaf ear to orders to quit the fighting in the streets. They failed to exploit, organize or issue specific instructions to those Group members who were members of the Control Patrols. They issued no orders to Máximo Franco, a Group member and delegate of the Rojinegra Column, which, along with the POUM division commanded by Rovira, had left the front line in order to intervene in the fighting in Barcelona. Both Josep Rovira and Máximo Franco were persuaded to return to the front by Isgleas, Abad de Santillán and Molina — that is, by the CNT personnel who gave the orders in the Generalidad's Defense Department. The Friends of Durruti trusted entirely to the creativity and instincts of the masses. There was not even the merest hint of coordination between the various members of the Group: instead everyone did as he pleased, wherever he thought he must or wherever seemed best to him. They failed to counter the action of the CNT leaders who toured the barricades to argue with and persuade the grassroots militants to quit the barricades.

And the CNT masses, bewildered by the appeals from their leaders (the very same leaders as on July 19!) eventually chose to give up the fight, even though, to begin with, they defied the CNT leadership's appeals for concord and for the fighting to cease for the sake of antifascist unity. On Tuesday May 6th, as a gesture of good will and to restore peace to the city, the militants of the CNT withdrew from the Telephone Exchange building where the fighting had begun: it was immediately occupied by the security forces and UGT members took up the work stations. When anarchist leaders protested, the Generalidad's response was that "it was a matter of a *fait accompli*" and the CNT leaders chose not to broadcast this further "treachery," lest it inflame passions.

The Friends of Durruti Group was at no time a serious impediment to the CNT's policy of antifascist unity. At most they were an opposition critical of the CNT and FAI leaderships, and above all, an irksome and unwelcome reminder that the policy of collaboration with the machinery of the State was a betrayal of anarcho-syndicalist principles and ideology.

Distribution of the handbill around the barricades was no easy undertaking, risking the suspicions of many militants and even braving physical[18] retaliation.

We know of one meeting between Balius and Josep Rebull, the secretary of the POUM's Cell 72, during the May events. A meeting which, given the numerical slightness of both organizations, had no practical effect. The Friends of Durruti declined Josep Rebull's suggestion that they issue a joint Manifesto.[19]

The Manifesto which the Group distributed on May 8th,[20] in which they reviewed the May events, was printed on the presses of *La Batalla*. The Group, having been denounced by the CNT as a band of provocateurs, had no presses on which to print it. A POUM militian by the name of Paradell, a leader of the Shop assistants' union, upon discovering the problem facing the Friends of Durruti Group, raised the matter with Josep Rebull, the administrator of the POUM newspaper, and the latter, honoring his basic duty of revolutionary solidarity, and without consultation with any higher party authority, offered the use of his presses to the Friends of Durruti Group.[21]

In the Manifesto, the Friends of Durruti linked the seizure of the Telephone Exchange with earlier provocations. They named the Esquerra Republicana, the PSUC, and the Generalidad's armed agencies as responsible for having triggered the May events. The Friends of Durruti asserted the revolutionary character of July 1936 (and argued that it was not just opposition to a fascist uprising) and of May 1937 (which was not simply aimed at a change of government):

> Our Group which was on the street, on the barricades, defending the proletariat's gains, calls for the total triumph of the social revolution. We cannot countenance the fiction, and the counterrevolutionary fact, whereby a new government is formed with the same parties, but with different representatives.

The Friends of Durruti countered the parliamentary compromises which they labeled as deceit with their revolutionary program, as set out in that handbill distributed on May 5th:

> Our Group demands the immediate establishment of a revolutionary junta, the shooting of the guilty ones, the disarming of the armed corps, the socialization of the economy and the disbanding of all the political parties which turned on the working class.

The Friends of Durruti Group had no hesitation in arguing that the battle had been won by the workers and, that being so, they had to do away once and for all with a Generalidad that signified nothing. The Group leveled a charge of **treason** against the CNT's committees and leaders who had brought the victorious workers' uprising to a standstill:

> The Generalidad stands for nothing. Its continued existence bolsters the counterrevolution. We workers have carried the day. It defies belief that the CNT's committees should have acted with such timidity that they ventured to order a 'cease-fire' and indeed forced a return to work when we stood on the very threshold of total victory. No account was taken of the provenance of the attack no heed paid to the true meaning of the present events. Such conduct has to be described as treason to the revolution which no one ought to commit or encourage in the name of anything. And we know how to categorize the noxious work carried out by *Solidaridad Obrera* and the CNT's most prominent militants."

The description "treason" was repeated in a reference to the CNT Regional Committee's disavowal of the Friends of Durruti, and to the transfer of responsibilities for security and defense (not those under Generalidad control, but the ones under CNT control) to the central government in Valencia:

> The treason is on a monumental scale. The two essential guarantees of the working class, security and defense, are offered to our enemies on a platter.

The Manifesto closed with a short self-criticism of some tactical shortcomings during the May events, and an optimistic look to the future — one which the immediate tide of repression unleashed on May 28 would show to be vain and insubstantial. May 1937 did not end in stalemate, but was a heavy defeat for the proletariat.

For all of the mythology surrounding the events of May 1937, the fact is that it represented a very chaotic, confused[22] situation, characterized by every one of the sides involved in the fighting developing an enthusiasm for negotiations. May 1937 was not at all a revolutionary insurrection, but began as a defense of "trade union ownership" established in July 1936. What triggered the fighting was the storming of the Telephone Exchange by Generalidad security troops. And that move was part and parcel of the Companys's government's ongoing intent to recover, bit by bit, the powers which the "irregular" situation of a workers' uprising in July 19 had **momentarily** had wrested from it. The recent successes scored in Puigcerdá and throughout the Cerdaña paved the way for a definitive move in Barcelona and right across Catalonia. It is obvious that Companys felt that he had the backing of Comorera (PSUC) and Antonov-Ovseenko (the Soviet consul) with whom he had worked very closely and to great effect since December, when the POUM had been dropped from the

Generalidad government. Stalinist policy coincided with Companys's aims: the undermining and side-lining of revolutionary forces, that is, of the POUM and the CNT, were Soviet aims that could only be encompassed if the bourgeois Generalidad government could be strengthened. The protracted crisis opened up in the Generalidad government following the CNT's refusal to accept the March 4, 1937 decree disbanding the Control Patrols, was resolved with violence (after several instances of armed skirmishing in Vilanesa, La Fatarella, Cullera (Valencia), Bellver, and at Roldan Cortada's funeral, etc.) in the attack upon the Telephone Exchange and in the bloody events of May in Barcelona. Stultifying shortsightedness, unshakable fidelity to antifascist unity and the extent of the main anarcho-syndicalist leaders' (from Peiró to Federica Montseny, from Abad de Santillán to Garcia Oliver, from Marianet to Valerio Mas) collaboration with the republican government, were not negligible factors, nor had the Generalidad government and Soviet agents overlooked them. They could also count upon an asinine saintliness, as was amply demonstrated during the May events.

As far as the actions of the Friends of Durruti Group during the May events are concerned, a misleading mythologization of its role on the barricades and its handbill[23] would also be out of place. As we have stated already, the Friends of Durruti did not, at any time, intend to unseat the CNT leadership, but contented themselves to the utterance of scathing criticisms of its leaders and their policy of treason towards the revolution. Maybe they were unable to do anything else, given their numbers and the slightness of their influence upon the CNT's mass following. But we should single out their involvement in the street-fighting,[24] their ascendancy on several barricades on the Ramblas, especially ones opposite their headquarters,[25] and their involvement in the fighting in Sants, La Torrassa and Sallent. Naturally, their attempts to offer a lead and some minimal political demands in the handbill of May 5, 1937 deserve to be emphasized. Distribution of that handbill was no easy undertaking and cost several Group members their lives. In the distribution of it around the barricades, they could depend upon help from CNT militants. Among the activities during the May events worth mentioning, we should not forget the call, issued by Balius from a barricade located at the junction of the Ramblas and the Calle Hospital, for all of Europe's workers to show solidarity with the Spanish revolution.[26] Upon receiving reports that a Column of Assault Guards was on its way from Valencia to put down the revolt, the Friends of Durruti responded by trying to marshal an anarchist column to head it off. But this never got beyond the planning stages, in that it was not taken up by the CNT militants who set about abandoning their barricades.

Finally, we ought to single out, from a political point or view, the agreement reached with the POUM that an appeal should be issued to the workers that they should seek, before quitting the barricades, assurances that there would be no retaliation: and above all pointing out that retention of arms — which ought never to be surrendered — constituted the best guarantee of all.

From a theoretical angle, the Friends of Durruti's role was much more outstanding after the May events when they set about publishing their newspaper, which borrowed its name from the paper published by Marat during the French Revolution: *The People's Friend.*

Notes for Chapter 6.

1. Information about the May events has been taken from the following sources:

J. Arquer *Les Jornades de maig* Unpublished manuscript deposited with the AHN in Madrid

Burnett Bolloten *La Guerra civil española: Revolución y contrarrevolución* (Alianza Editorial, Madrid, 1989, pp. 659-704) [English language readers should see Burnett Bolloten, *The Spanish Revolution*, Chapel Hill, 1979]

Luis Companys "This is a carbon copy of notes made by President . . . and of teletyped conversations between various political figures during the fighting in Barcelona, May 3-7, 1937" [Deposited with the Hoover Institution]

Manuel Cruells *Mayo sangriento. Barcelona 1937* (Ed. Juventud, Barcelona, 1970)

Francisco Lacruz *El alzamiento, la revolución y el terror en Barcelona* (Libreria Arysel, Barcelona, 1943)

Frank Mintz and Manuel Peciña *Los Amigos de Durruti, los trotsquistas y los sucesos de mayo* (Campo Abierto, Madrid, 1978)

Andres Nin "El problema de los órganos de poder en la revolución española." Published in French in No. 1 of *Juillet. Revue internationale du POUM* in June 1937. Available in a Spanish translation in *Balance* No. 2 (March 1994)

Hugo Oehler *Barricades in Barcelona* (1937). Reprinted in *Revolutionary History* No. 2, (1988) pp. 22-29

George Orwell "Yo fui tesligo en Barcelona" in *Boletin de información sobre el proceso politico contra el POUM* No. 5, Barcelona, December 15, 1937

[Agustin Souchy] *Los sucesos en Barcelona, Relación documental de las trágicas jornadas de la 1a de semana Mayo de 1937* (Ediciones Españolas Ebro, no place indicated, 3rd edition August 1937)

Pavel and Clara Thalmann *Combats pur la liberté. Moscou, Madrid, Paris* (Spartacus, Paris, 1983)

Various *Los sucesos de mayo de 1937. ona revolución en la Republica* (Fundació Andreu Nin, Barcelona 1988)
Various *Sucesos de mayo (1937) Cuadernos de la guerra civil* No. 1, (Fundación Salvador Segui, Madrid, 1987)
2. Jordi Arquer *Les jornades de maig* Unpublished manuscript text deposited with the AHN in Madrid.
3. The Councilor for defense was CNT member Francisco Isgleas, a faithful friend and supporter of Garcia Oliver, who, during the May events, played a very prominently "neutral" role, preventing CNT and POUM troops from taking a hand in the fighting. Miguel Caminal offers testimony from Rafael Vidiella, according to whom Companys ordered Artemi Aiguadé to take the Telephone Exchange, and this in the presence of several councilors and the CNT's Domenech, who merely pointed out the possible consequences of such a move. [In Miguel Caminal *Joan Comorera* Vol. II, p. 120]
4. See Arquer, op. cit. and a report in *Solidaridad Obrera* of May 2, 1937 of the Generalidad council's having met on Saturday May 1.
5. Yet Arquer (op. cit.) appears to believe that Aiguadé was acting off his own bat, without the knowledge of the panel. Be that as it may, it seems obvious that the Generalidad government had washed its hands of Tarradellas's policy of compromise and collaboration and opted instead for the direct confrontation (as advocated by Companys) which had worked so well in Bellver de Cerdaña.
6. See the observations of Manuel Cruells (*Mayo sangriento. Barcelona 1937* Ed. Juventud, Barcelona 1970, pp. 55-56) on this point. Cruells was a journalist with the *Diari de Barcelona* at the time. As for the influence of Stalinists over Aiguadé or Rodriguez Salas, whether there was any or not strikes us as irrelevant given that collaboration that was obtained between Companys, Comorera and the Soviet consul in Barcelona. This view is also expressed by Agustin Souchy in *Los sucesos de Barcelona. Relación* . . . op. cit. p. 13.
7. Shortly after news broke of the armed clash inside the Telephone Exchange building: "In order to ensure that this incident would not lead to wider clashes, the Chief of Service at the Public Order Commissariat, Eroles, the general secretary of the 'Control Patrols,' Asens and Diaz, representing the Defense Committee, traveled to the Telephone Exchange to get the attackers to withdraw. Rodriguez Salas consulted by telephone with Aiguadé, the Councilor for Internal Security, on whose orders he had acted, and the latter instructed him that under no circumstances was he to withdraw, but should hold the positions he had captured. . . .
Along with some other anarchists, Valerio Mas showed up at the office of [. . .] Tarradellas, asking him to order the Assault Guards trying to occupy the Telephone Exchange to withdraw [. . .] Tarradellas, and later [. . .] Arlemio Aiguadé,

on whom they also called, feigned surprise and claimed that they had not issued any instructions to the effect that the Telephone Exchange should be occupied.
—This is Rodriguez Salas acting on his own account — Aiguadé told them. — And I promise you that [. . .] I will issue the requisite "orders for peace to be restored."
[From Francisco Lacruz *El Alzamiento, la revolución y el terror en Barcelona* (Libreria Arysel, Barcelona, 1943)]
Francisco Lacruz's information was probably lifted from the pamphlet published anonymously by Agustin Souchy in 1937 which stated: "To ensure that this incident would not lead to wider clashes, the police chief Eroles, the Control Patrols' general secretary Asens, and comrade Diaz, representing the Defense Committee, journeyed to the Telephone Exchange [. . .] Valerio Mas, along with some other comrades, spoke to the premier, Tarradellas and the councilor of the Interior, Aiguadé, to urge them to pull out the troops. [. . .] Tarradellas [. . .] and Aiguadé assured them that they knew nothing of what had happened at the Telephone Exchange. It was discovered later that Aiguadé himself had signed the order for it to be occupied." [*Los sucesos de Barcelona. Relación*. . . op. cit. p. 12]
8. See the claims of Julián Gorkin in "Reúnion du sous-secretariat international du POUM — 14 mai 1937": "In point of fact the movement was entirely spontaneous. Of course, that very relative spontaneity ought to be explained: since July 19th, *Defense Committees*, organized primarily by rank and file CNT and FAI personnel, had been formed pretty well everywhere in Barcelona and across Catalonia. For a time, these Committees were scarcely active, yet it can be said that it was they which mobilized the working class on May 3. They were the action groups behind the movement. We know that no general strike instructions went out from either of the two trade union associations."
9. Jordi Arquer *Història de la fundació i actuació de la 'Agrupació Amigos de Durruti'* Unpublished manuscript [Deposited with the Hoover Institution]
10. Ibid.
11. Jordi Arquer, op. cit.
There can be no question but that Nin took an interest in the Friends of Durruti right from their launch, since as early as March 4, 1937, in *La Batalla*, Nin published an article fulsome in its praises for the ideas mooted by Jaime Balius in an article printed in *La Noche* of March 2, 1937, in which he warned of the dangers of the counterrevolution's steady progress in Catalonia.
12. On May 3rd, the CNT Regional Committee and the POUM's Executive Committee met in the Casa CNT-FAI for talks about the situation. After lengthy and detailed analysis of the prospects for action on the part of the POUMists, Valerio Mas, on behalf of the CNT Regional Committee, thanked

Nin, Andrade and Solano for a pleasant evening, reiterating several times that the debate and discussion had been highly interesting, and that they should do it again some time. But no agreement was reached or made. The shortsightedness and political ineptitude of the CNT personnel defied belief: they thought that it was enough that they should have bared their teeth, that the barricades had to come down now, because the Stalinists and Republicans, having tested the strength of the CNT, would not dare go beyond that. On making his way back to the Ramblas, and dodging the barricades, Andrade could not help repeating over and over to himself: "A pleasant evening! A pleasant evening!" [Oral evidence taken from Wilebaldo Solano, Barcelona June 16, 1994]

On the meeting between a POUM delegation made up of Nin, Andrade, Gorkin, Bonet and Solano and the CNT Regional Committee, and, more especially, with its secretary, Valerio Mas, see Wilebaldo Solano "La Juventud Comunista Iberica (POUM) en las jornadas de mayo de 1937 en Barcelona" in L*s sucesos de mayo de 1937, Una revolución en la Republica* (Fundación Nin y Fundación Segui, Pandola Libros, Barcelona, 1988, pp. 158-160)

13. Jordi Arquer, op. cit. See also Wilebaldo Solano, op. cit.

14. Jordi Arquer, op. cit. See also *La Batalla* editorials in Nos. 235 (May 6, 1937) 236 (May 7, 1937) and 237 (May 8, 1937)

15. According to the Thalmanns' account. See Note 1 above.

16. Wilebaldo Solano, op. cit. p. 164

17. The Barcelona Local Committee (of the POUM) "Informe de la actuación del Comité local durante los dias de mayo que ésta presenta a discusión de las celulas de Barcelona," Archivo Histórico Naciónal de Madrid.

18. According to Balius's own claims in his correspondence with Burnett Bolloten, distributing the handbill on the barricades cost several Group members their lives.

For the printing and distribution of the handbill, see Pavel and Clara Thalmann *Combats pour la liberte. Moscou, Madrid, Paris* (Spartacus, Paris, 1983, pp. 189-191)

19. Josep Rebull's answer No. 7 to a questionnaire put to him by Agustin Guillamón (Banyuls-sur-mer, December 16, 1985):

> Question: Did Cell 72 attempt to establish contacts with other groups with an eye to creating a revolutionary front, that is to say, with the Friends of Durruti, the Libertarian Youth, Balius, Munis, or other segments of the POUM?
>
> Josep Rebull: The only contact with the 'Friends of Durruti' came during the May events, but the numerical slightness of that group, which had no links with the rank and file, and the modest

representativity of Cell 72 did not produce a practical agreement, such as we wished to suggest, that we issue a manifesto to the struggling workers.

20. Balius slated in 1971: "on account of the 'cease-fire' order issued by the CNT's ministers, we issued a manifesto describing the committees responsible for that order as 'traitors and cowards.' That manifesto was distributed throughout the Catalan capital by the members of the Group and by the Libertarian Youth [Jaime Balius "Por los fueros de la verdad" in *Le Combat syndicaliste* of September 2, 1971]

21. Jordi Arquer, op. cit.

22. See Juan Andrade *Notas sobre la guerra civil (Actuación del POUM)* (Ediciones Libertarias, Madrid, 1986, pp. 117-125)

23. Because they puncture all the mythology, Andrade's comments upon the Friends of Durruti are extremely interesting: "[. . .] we made contact with the 'Friends of Durruti', a group of which it has to be said that they did not amount to much, being a lightweight circle which had no intention of doing anything more than act as an opposition within the FAI, and was in no way disposed to engage in concerted action with 'authoritarian marxists' like us. I am making this point because an attempt has since been made to depict the 'Friends of Durruti' as a mightily representative organization, articulating the revolutionary consciousness of the CNT-FAI. In reality, they counted for nothing organizationally and were a monument of confusion in ideological terms: they had no very precise idea of what they wanted and what they loved was ultra-revolutionary talk with no political impact, provided always that they involved no commitment to action and did not breach FAI discipline. We did all that we could, in spite of everything, to come to some agreement on the situation, but I believe we only managed to jointly sign one of two manifestoes urging resistance, because they would not countenance anything more. Later the group vanished completely and found no public expression." [in Juan Andrade, op. cit. 12]

In any event, Andrade's claims are, to say the least, contradictory, since one is forced to wonder why the POUM bothered to have talks with the Friends of Durruti if they amounted to nothing and were nobodies. Then again, we have already pointed to the interest which Nin displayed in Balius's stance and in the birth of the Friends of Durruti, from as early as March 1937. Similarly, there is no question but that Andrade of 1986 contradicts the Andrade of 1937 who wrote the article "CNT-POUM" carried by *La Batalla* on May 1, 1936: see Chapter 5, note 5.

24. As Balius himself was at pains to make clear, the Friends of Durruti were alone [only the Group and the Bolshevik-Leninist Section issued leaflets with

revolutionary watchwords] in welcoming the street-fighting and they attempted to provide the spontaneous struggle of the workers during the events of May 1937 with a lead and revolutionary purpose: "In *Espoir*, Floreal Castillo states that Camillo Berneri was the leader of the opposition in May. This is wrong. Camillo Berneri published *La Lutte de Classes* [actually, it was the Italian language paper *Guerra di classe,*] but played no active role. It was the men from the Friends of Durruti who turned up the heat. It was the miners of Sallent who erected the barricade on the Ramblas at the junction with the Calle Hospital, beside our beloved Group's headquarters." [Jaime Balius "Por los fueros de la verdad" in *Le Combat syndicaliste* of September 2, 1971]
Balius's testimony is corroborated by Jaume Miravithes: "The city — so far as I know — is occupied throughout by FAI personnel, especially by groups from the Friends of Durruti, and by relatively large numbers from the POUM." [Jaume Miravithes *Episodis de la guerra civil espanyola. Notes del meus arxius (2)* (Pórtic, Barcelona, 1972, p. 144)]

25. As Balius says in his article "Por los fueros de la verdad," cited earlier, the barricade was built by miners from Sallent.

26. See Pablo Ruiz "Elogio póstumo de Balius" in *Le Combat syndicaliste/ Solidaridad Obrera* of January 9, 1981.

7. After May

The CNT leadership moved that members of the Friends of Durruti Group be expelled, but it never could get that measure ratified by any assembly of unions.[1] The CNT membership sympathized with the revolutionary opposition embodied in the Group. Not that this means that they subscribed either to the activities or the thinking of Friends of Durruti, but they did understand their stance and respected, indeed supported, their criticisms of the CNT leadership.[2]

The CNT leadership deliberately used and abused the allegation "marxist," which was the worst conceivable term of abuse among anarchists and one that was repeatedly used against the Group and more specifically against Balius. There is nothing in the Group's theoretical tenets, much less in the columns of *El Amigo del Pueblo*, or in their various manifestoes and handbills to merit the description "marxist" being applied to the Group. They were simply an opposition to the CNT leadership's collaborationist policy, making their stand within the organization and upon anarcho-syndicalist ideology. The first issue of *El Amigo del Pueblo* was published lawfully on May 19,[3] many of its galley proofs erased by the censors. The red and black broad sheet cover page carried a drawing showing a smiling Durruti holding the red and black flag aloft. Number 1 bore no date. The editorial and administrative offices were listed as No. 1, first floor, Rambla de las Flores. The paper proclaimed itself the mouthpiece of the Friends of Durruti. Balius was listed as editor-in-chief, and Eleuterio Roig, Pablo Ruiz and Domingo Paniagua as editors. The most intriguing article which bore Balius's signature was entitled "For the record. We are not agents provocateurs," in which Balius deplored the insults and aspersions emanating from the CNT's own ranks. He mentioned the handbill and the manifesto issued in May, claiming that he had not reprinted these because they would assuredly and inevitably have been censored. He directly attacked *Solidaridad Obrera*[4] for its venomous attitude towards the Friends of Durruti and refuted the slurs emanating from the CNT leadership: "We are not agents provocateurs."

No. 2, which displays no censored passages, had a print run of fifteen thousand copies.[5] The colored cover page showed a drawing commemorating Ascaso's death in the attack upon the Atarazanas barracks. This issue was date-lined Barcelona, Wednesday May 26, 1937. The cover bore the following notice:

> The squalid treatment which the censors have meted out to us requires us to give it the slip. The impertinence of erasing our most insignificant remarks is a shame and a disgrace. We cannot, nor will we put up with it. Slaves, no!

Consequently, this edition was not presented for censorship and was published clandestinely.[6] Prominent in this issue was the denunciation of the watchwords issued by the UGT, the Stalinist-controlled union which had expelled the POUMists from its ranks and asked that the CNT treat the Friends of Durruti likewise. It carried no article with Balius's byline. However, two articles stand out, not so much on account of any intrinsic worth but rather on account of the mentality they mirror. One of them, signed by "Fulmen" drew parallels between the French Revolution of 1793 and the Spanish revolution in 1937, between Marat and Balius and between the Jabobins and the **durrutistas**. Another, uncredited article denounced a series of leading Catalanist personalities living in Paris on retainers from the Generalidad. A comparison was also made in a populist, demagogic way, between the salaries received by Companys and other politicians and the pay of militians and the difficulties of raising funds to keep the war going. Both these articles are interesting, in that they indicate a workerist, demagogic outlook, which seems to have tied in very well with the day-to-day economic straits and discomforts of the common people, and which was not commonly found in the rest of the newspapers of the time. This, we may say, was a characteristic feature of *El Amigo del Pueblo*. This edition's editorial comment, which was carried on the back cover under the title "The Negrin government," bemoaned the formation of a counter-revolutionary government under Communist Party sponsorship as a result of the May events, the short-term objective of it being to disarm the working class and form a bourgeois army. The editorial categorized the resolution of the crisis in the Valencia government as a clear example of colonial intervention [Russian intervention, it was implied]. Balius was jailed and refused bail (around mid-June) over this editorial, although he was never brought to trial, since the Tribunal charged with hearing the case ordered him released. A fortnight after that release, (around mid-October) he was jailed again (at the start of November) for two months, under a preventive detention order, and handed over to Commissioner Burillo.[7] Thus he was incarcerated for some nine months in all and only escaped a third period behind bars because he fled Barcelona to avoid it.

Issue No. 3 bore the date June 12, 1937, claimed to have been published in Barcelona and was now entirely without color. This issue seemed a lot more pugnacious, and the articles had a lot more bite to them. There were denunciations of the murder of several anarchist militants, encroachments against the Control Patrols which it was intended to outlaw, and the text of their May handbill was quoted and its content explained. It was announced as imminent events crucial to the future of the revolution, which was in immediate danger.[8] There was an uncredited article, ascribable to Fulmen, on the French Revolution: news of the military successes of the anarchist Cipriano Mera on the Madrid front: some poems by Eleuterio Roig: an article by Santana Calero in which he averred that imitating Durruti meant not appeasement, but rather, advocacy of the latter's ideological positions on the necessity of winning the war if they were to be free: Durruti's radio broadcast from the Madrid front was reprinted: there was a demagogic article on the Aragon front and the rearguard: a scathing denunciation of the latest statements by Peiró regarding the introduction of a republic like the one in existence prior to July 19 : and above all, most interestingly of all, an article entitled "Apropos of the May Events" in which the Friends of Durruti retracted the description "traitors" used in their Manifesto of May 8th about the CNT's leading committees, and simultaneously asked that the description "agents provocateurs" used about the Friends of Durruti by the CNT be retracted too.

In issue No. 4, dated June 22, 1937, there was a report of Balius's having been detained without bail. Prominently displayed on the cover was the Group's schedule of demands (already re-vamped several times since it had first appeared in the manifesto issued in late March 1937), which proposed draconian measures like compulsory unionization, purges of the rearguard, rationing, arming of the proletariat, disbanding of the agencies of repression, etc. . . . aimed at defending a revolution menaced by the reaction, and winning the war against the fascists:

> We, 'irresponsible agents provocateurs,' call for: trade union direction of economic and social life. The free municipality.

The army and public order to be overseen by the working class.

Dissolution of the Armed Corps. Retention of the Defense Committees and Defense Councilorships.

Arms must be in the possession of the proletariat. Rifles are the ultimate guarantee of the revolution's gains. No one but the working class may have access to them. Abolition of ranks. Fortifications battalions to be made up of the Proletariat's enemies.

Compulsory unionization. Employment bureaus. An end to references in securing employment. Ration cards. Obligatory labor. The rearguard must live for the war.

Socialization of all the means of production and exchange. A fight to the death against fascism and its accomplices. Purging of the rearguard. Establishment of neighborhood committees.

Immediate introduction of the family wage, with no bureaucratic exceptions. The war and the revolution must touch us all equally. Suspension of the bourgeois Parliament. Suspension of passports.

Mobilization against the counterrevolution.

Absolute non-compliance with the coercive measures of the State, such as enforcement of censorship, disarming of the workers, State confiscation of radio stations, etc.

Resolute opposition to Municipalization of the means of production until such time as the working class enjoys absolute mastery of the country.

Reversion to our organizations' revolutionary tenor in full.

Utter opposition to governmental collaboration, it being utterly counter-productive in the emancipation of the proletariat.

War to the death against speculators, bureaucrats and those behind the rise in the cost of living. On a war footing against any armistice.

On page 2, the following announcement or reminder appeared: "Revolutionary Program of the Friends of Durruti Group:

A revolutionary junta.

Economic power to the unions. Free municipalities.

We want to step up a gear. We are anarchists."

In addition, there was the customary poem from Eleuterio Roig, the usual article by Fulmen on the French Revolution, and a piece by Santana Calero urging the Libertarian youth and the FAI to get to work in the trade unions and reaffirming the need to win the war and prosecute the revolution simultaneously. Of course, outstanding was a memorable article by Jaime Balius entitled "In self-defense. I require an explanation." In this article, Balius defended himself against the charge that he was a marxist, a charge leveled at him by the CNT leaders and CNT press as the most wounding insult of all.

In issue No. 5 of *El Amigo del Pueblo*, dated July 20, 1937, and printed in a smaller format, the same address is given for the paper's administration and editorial offices as in the very first issue, even though the Group's offices had been shut down by the police and the newspaper was being printed clandestinely. This was part of a ploy to throw police inquiries off the scent. They thought that El *Amigo del Pueblo* was probably being printed in France by then, in Perpignan or in Montpellier, with the help of French anarchists, although in fact it was still being published in Barcelona. Starting with this edition, and in all succeeding issues of *El Amigo del Pueblo,* all articles were unsigned, except for the occasional one published under an alias. At no time did Balius allow his imprisonment to interfere with his contributing to editorials, sometimes even writing articles from prison.

Issue No. 5 is one of the most interesting of the *El Amigo del Pueblo* series. Page one carries an editorial entitled "A revolutionary theory." **That article alone would be enough to highlight the political and historical importance of the Friends of Durruti,** not just in relation to the history of the civil war, but in anarchist ideology. In the editorial, the Friends of Durruti ascribed the progress of the counterrevolution and the failure of the CNT, following its incontrovertible, absolute triumph in July 1936, to one single factor: lack of a revolutionary program. And this had also been behind the defeat in May 1937. The conclusion to which they had come is spelled out with tremendous clarity:

> the downward spiral [of the revolution] must be attributed exclusively to the absence of a specific program and short-term achievements, and to the fact that, on this score, we have fallen into the snares of counterrevolutionary sectors just when circumstances were plainly taking a favorable turn as far as meeting the proletariat's aspirations was concerned. And by failing to give free rein to July's awakening along plainly class lines, we have rendered possible petit bourgeois rule which could

> never ever have come about, had a unanimous determination to place the proletariat in the driving seat in this country prevailed.
>
> [. . .] making the blunder of thinking that a revolution of the social type could share its economic and social dynamics with enemy sectors. [. . .]
>
> In May the problem was posed anew. Once again the talk was of supremacy in the direction of the revolution. But the very same persons who, in July, took fright at the danger of foreign intervention, come the events of May, displayed a lack of vision which culminated in that baleful 'cease-fire' which, later, despite a truce's having been agreed, translated as an ongoing disarmament and ruthless repression of the working class. [. . .]
>
> So that, by denying ourselves a program, which is to say, libertarian communism, we surrender ourselves entirely to our adversaries, who did and still do have a program and guidelines [. . .] to the petit-bourgeois parties which ought to have been stamped out in July and in May. In our view, any other sector, had it enjoyed an absolute majority such as we possessed, would have set itself up as absolute master of the situation.
>
> In the preceding edition of our newspaper we spelled out a program. We are alive to the necessity for a revolutionary junta, for the unions to have control of the economy and for the Municipalities to organize freely. Our Group has sought to trace a path, for fear lest circumstances similar to July and May, might see us perform the same way. And success lies in the existence of a program which must be unwaveringly backed by rifles [. . .]
>
> Revolutions without theory fail to make progress. We of the 'Friends of Durruti' have outlined our thinking, which may be amended as appropriate in great social upheavals, but which hinges upon two essential points which cannot be avoided. A program, and rifles.

This is a crucial text, for it **represents a landmark in the evolution of anarchist thinking**. The theoretical notions set out here, previously sketched only in a very confused way, are now spelled out with dazzling clarity. And these theoretical acquisitions were later to be reiterated and thought through in Balius's pamphlet *Hacia una nueva revolución.* But here they appear for the first time. And no one can fail to appreciate the novelty and significance of them in the context of anarchist thought. The Friends of Durruti had picked up old theoretical concepts, at which they had arrived at the end of a painful historical experience, over a civil war and revolutionary process, which had starkly exposed the contradictions and demands of the class struggle. Are we to believe, then, that this evolution in the political thinking of the Friends of Durruti can seriously and verifiably be ascribed to the influence of some outside group, say, Trotskyists or POUMists? It is beyond dispute that **this is an evolution** attributable to the Friends of Durruti Group exclusively. In their analysis of the political and historical situation, they had come to the conclusion that, in a revolution, there was an ineluctable requirement that a Revolutionary Junta be established. Naturally, the Friends of Durruti shunned the characteristic terminology of marxism,[9] and employed a different idiom, characteristic of anarchist ideology: and that idiom in which they frame the notion of "dictatorship of the proletariat," is further proof that we are dealing here with evolution internal to the Group, rather than its being colonized or captivated by some outside group. Social and historical realities are stubborn enough and tough enough to ensure that the elements of revolutionary theory can germinate in a revolutionary group which simply keeps its eyes open and its mind alert.

In the same edition of the paper, there was an analysis of events since May, which included a denunciation of the incarceration and trial of POUM militants by the Stalinists, and the destruction of the collectives. Pointed contrasts were drawn between the ease in which the middle classes, the Stalinists' spawning ground, lived, and the persecution of revolutionary workers. There was also Fulmen's usual piece on the French Revolution, outlining an interesting contrast between the French revolutionary process and the Spanish. Finally, there was an outstanding long article denouncing abortive attempts on the part of the CNT's leading committees to have the Friends of Durruti expelled.

Issue No. 6 of *El Amigo del Pueblo* is dated Barcelona, August 12, 1937. The editorial is headed "Necessity of a Revolutionary Junta" reiterating the previous edition's editorial about the need for a revolutionary junta and arguing that a revolutionary junta ought to have been set up in July 1936:

> From the July movement we must conclude that the revolution's enemies must be ruthlessly crushed. This was one of the chief mistakes for which we are now paying with interest. This defensive mission will fall to the revolutionary Junta which must show the enemy no mercy. [. . .]
>
> The establishment of a revolutionary Junta is of capital importance. It is not a matter of yet another abstraction. It is the

> outcome of a series of failures and disasters. And is the categorical amendment of the trajectory followed hitherto.
>
> In July an antifascist committee was set up which was not equal to the implications of that sublime hour. How could the embryo thrown up by the barricades have developed, incorporating as it did the friends and foes of the revolution alike? The antifascist committee, with that make-up, was scarcely the embodiment of the fighting in July.[10]
>
> [. . .] we advocate that the only participants in the revolutionary Junta should be the workers of city and countryside and the combatants who have shown themselves, at every crucial juncture in the conflict, to be the champions of social revolution. [. . .]
>
> the 'Friends of Durruti Group' which knew enough to work out a precise critique of the May events is even now sensible of the need to establish a revolutionary Junta, along the lines we have in mind, and we regard it as indispensable for the defense of the revolution [. . .]

The evolution of the Friends of Durruti's political thinking was by now unstoppable. After the necessity of a dictatorship of the proletariat had been acknowledged, the next issue to arise was: And who is to exercise that dictatorship of the proletariat? The answer was: the revolutionary Junta, promptly defined as the vanguard of revolutionaries. And its role? We cannot believe that it can be anything other than the one which marxists ascribe to the revolutionary party.

However, in No. 2 of *La Voz Leninista,* Munis was critical of issue No 6 of *El Amigo del Pueblo* because he regarded its contents as a retreat from the same formulas devised by the Friends of Durruti Group during, and in the immediate aftermath of the May events.

Issue No. 6 also carried a report on the trial mounted against the POUM and on the murder of Nin, for which the government in place was held to be accountable: in addition to the customary article on the French Revolution, there were some others of lesser interest. On the back page there was a printer's stamp reading "Imp. Libertaria-Perpignan." There is every likelihood that this was a false trail laid for the police, for *El Amigo del Pueblo* was still being printed in Barcelona.[11]

Issue No. 7 of the newspaper was datelined Barcelona, September 31,[12] and there were several articles which stood out: on the repression unleashed in Aragon by the Stalinists in the wake of the dissolution of the Council of Aragon and the break-up of the anarchist collectives: rebutting the false allegations about the Friends of Durruti peddled by Agustin Souchy in an anonymous pamphlet published by Ediciones Ebro: opposing the re-introduction of freedom of religion: protesting at the unreasonable increase in basic living costs, etc. There was also an outstanding note of humor, very indicative of the times, which went as follows:

> We move the immediate expulsion from our Organization of persons by the name of Mikhail Bakunin, Peter Kropotkin, Sébastien Faure, Errico Malatesta and Ricardo Mella.
>
> By way of compensating for these expulsions, we move that a tribute be paid to the 'interventionists,' on account of their having successfully defeated the counterrevolutionary peril.
>
> Our 'orthodoxy renders us incompatible with those who furnish ideological and material sustenance to 'uncontrollables,' while it also fills us with admiration for the glorious 'infallibility' of the great interpreters of 'circumstance.'

The editorial analyzed the import of the May events, which the Friends of Durruti held to be an insurrection intended to remedy the mistakes made since July. It railed against the fence sitting by certain prominent anarchist militants whose resistance of "totalitarian temptations" amounted to nothing more than an abdication of the introduction of libertarian communism. Repeatedly, it was argued that anarchists had to learn the lessons of experience:

> Totalitarian solutions have been shunned. An official seal has been set upon the decision to refrain from establishing libertarian communism! The line which anarchism is to take — according to the declarations from comrades in positions of responsibility — is that no antifascist denomination should seek selfish advantage [. . .] Neither dictatorships nor democracies! it is argued. Where are we headed? Without a program of our own, we are in danger of remaining an appendage of bourgeois democracy and risk becoming the victims of any sector that operates with audacity. [. . .]
>
> Our present hour should be read exclusively in the light of past experience. If we persist in shutting our eyes to reality, which still stinks of the battlefield, the jails and the overall onslaught of the counterrevolution, we will be brutally driven out of the Peninsula.

> We may yet salvage the revolution. [. . .] Experience is a very hard taskmaster and from it we must deduce that we have to assert ourselves with the force of firepower and that we must annihilate those forces which are enemies of the working class and the revolution.
>
> Let us bear in mind the lessons of experience. Therein lies our salvation.

There was no plea for a *deus ex machina*: the Friends of Durruti were anarchists who had learned the lessons of the harshest firsthand experience. What novelties they introduced to anarchist theory may well have been old marxist postulates, themselves merely elementary lessons from the class struggle. But anyone who bandies about labels and regards that as having settled the matter is ill-advised. If the firsthand experience of the proletariat in the class struggle is not enough to remedy errors and if history has nothing to teach us from past struggles, we are left with an affirmation of the primacy of dogma and belief and a denial that there is any validity in experience and history.

The editorial in issue No. 8 of *El Amigo del Pueblo*, datelined Barcelona September 21, 1937, labored the need for a program if the revolution was to have any prospect of success. As with the ideas set out previously, it had nothing new to contribute. The remainder of the articles, which were fairly interesting, dealt with a variety of topics: food supplies, opposition to nationalist commemoration of the feast of September 11, the Aragon front, Angel Pestaña's return to the CNT fold.

In issue No. 9, dated October 20, 1937 carried an interesting manifesto, rehearsing the history of their origins and revolutionary action, as well as a programmatic inventory of the Group's political standpoints; this proved very controversial and was much commented upon, so much so that issue No. 10, dated November 8, 1937, carried an editorial defending it. The same edition greeted the appearance of *Alerta*, described as an ideologically kindred newspaper. There was unmistakable venom towards Comorera, who was savagely criticized for his policy as the man in charge of supplies, and for having dismissed the fighters of July 19 as "tribesmen." There was a report that Balius had been jailed again "following a period at liberty that has lasted barely fifteen or twenty days"[13]: he was convicted as the editor of *El Amigo del Pueblo* which was condemned as a clandestine newspaper in that it had refused to present itself for censorship since issue No. 2. The most interesting articles were entitled "We must speak plainly" and "An historic juncture." In humorous tones, it rebutted the usual charges hurled by the CNT at members of the Group who were labeled as "uncontrollables, provocateurs and counterrevolutionaries." After defending the Group's members and rehearsing their revolutionary and combat credentials, the article very tellingly declined to level any charges against the CNT and the FAI, on the grounds that "that would poison the waters of the spring from which we all must drink." Plain in this article is the Friends of Durruti's tremendously limited vision of their own fight. They confined themselves to gentle carping about the "wayward" leaders of the CNT and counted their avoidance of expulsion from the unions as their ultimate achievement. Their view was that, sooner or later, the two divergent strands of anarcho-syndicalism would have to come together, for, otherwise, they could not avoid being crushed by Stalinist dictatorship. It was plain from this article that the Group was drifting further and further from the radicalized stances it had struck in May. The second article deserving of comment, "An historic juncture," analyzed the unfavorable course of the war, as signaled by the fascists' uninterrupted victorious advance and their foreign backing. The Friends of Durruti wondered why whole provinces like Malaga or the North had been surrendered without their stores, industries or foodstuffs — which provided booty for the enemy — having been destroyed. The Group noted that the war on the Aragon front had been lost because of the central government's withholding of arms, because those arms would have gone to the CNT. The war effort was beset by treachery, because the officer class had not been purged, and because there was no fighting moral in the rearguard, and because bourgeois politicians had no thought for anything other than amassing a tidy fortune abroad. The Friends of Durruti called upon workers to win the war, and this call boiled down to the following ten points:

1. Establishment of a Revolutionary Junta.
2. All economic power to the unions.
3. Socialization of production and consumption.
4. Introduction of the producer's cart.
5. **Mobilization of the entire population.**
6. **Purging of the rearguard.**
7. Workers' control of the army.
8. The family wage. Abolition of all privileges.
9. Free municipality. Public order to be placed in workers' hands.
10. Rationing of consumption across the board.

This, though, was merely a list of demands. There was no hint as to how they might be achieved, nor of the tactics to be employed in order to campaign for them. So it was merely the exposition of a theoretical program for winning the war, a program beyond the Group's actual powers to implement, one which it in any case was not proposing seriously, but only as a propaganda or lobbying ploy. But direction of the war, or control of the army, or socialization of the economy, or control of public order could scarcely be mere demands: because power is not sued for, but seized. Consequently, we may claim that the Group was, at this point, far removed from playing any real part. It seemed to have run out of steam: and was becoming a mere shadow of its former self. The program, the demands, which may have been valid prior to May, were now a sad caricature and testified to the Group's utter powerlessness in a situation which had become thoroughly counterrevolutionary.

Issue No. 11 of *El Amigo del Pueblo* was dated November 20, 1937, the anniversary of Durruti's death and was almost entirely given over to commemorating that popular anarchist hero. Among the articles commenting with more or less success upon the person of Durruti, the most outstanding was undoubtedly the one entitled "Commenting on Durruti," in which *Solidaridad Obrera* was taken to task over Durruti's ideology and intentions. According to the author of the piece, *Soli* was arguing that Durruti had been ready to abjure every revolutionary principle for the sake of success in the war. The writer in *El Amigo del Pueblo* saw this contention as wrong-headed and the worst possible insult that could have been offered to Durruti's memory. The version of Durruti's ideology[14] offered by the Group was the very opposite of the one proffered by *Soli* :

> Durruti at no time abjured the revolution. While he did say that we had to abjure everything save victory, what he meant was that we had to be ready to face the greatest privation, and to lose our very lives, rather than let fascism defeat us.
>
> But in Durruti's mouth, the notion of victory does not imply the slightest dissociation of the war and the revolution. [. . .] We do not believe — and of this we are certain — that Durruti was arguing that the class which had won everything at the cost of the greatest sacrifices should be the one to give ground constantly and compromise to the advantage of the adversary class. [. . .]
>
> Durruti was keen to win the war, but he had his sights on the rearguard. [. . .] Buenaventura Durruti never forswore the revolution. Nor do we, the Friends of Durruti, forswear it.

No. 12 of *El Amigo del Pueblo*, dated February 1, 1938, carried a prominent editorial: "All power to the unions," expounding upon that particular point in the Group's program. There were various items on the battle for Teruel, urban transport and Montjuic prison, speculation in the food sector and the corruption obtaining on the borders.

No. 12 was probably the last issue of *El Amigo del Pueblo* . However, Jordi Arquer, in his short history of the Friends of Durruti argues that a total of 15 issues saw publication; and Balius, in his letter of June 10, 1946 to Burnett Bolloten, says that it published right to the end of 1938. Our supposition is based upon Balius's claim in the foreword to the English edition of that pamphlet, *Towards a Fresh Revolution* that the Group's final gathering took place after publication of that pamphlet. Given that No. 12 of *El Amigo del Pueblo* mentions the recent publication of *Towards* . . . we may conclude that following publication of the pamphlet in January 1938, and of No. 12 of the Group's press mouthpiece on February 1, 1938, the Group held its final meeting and to all intents carried out no further activity for the remainder of the war. This supposition is in any case borne out by the swingeingly effective repression that made life impossible for any revolutionary group. In January 1938, Fosco fled to France to escape arrest. February 13, 1938 saw the capture of the Bolshevik-Leninist Section by police, along with the arrest of the printer Baldomero Palau, from whose printshop *La Voz Leninista* and *El Amigo del Pueblo* was published. On April 19 the underground committee of POUM (José Rovira, Jordi Arquer, Oltra Picó, José Rodés, Maria Teresa Garcia Banús, Juan Farré Gassó, Wilebaldo Solano, etc.) was arrested.

Later, in the 1960s, a second series of *El Amigo del Pueblo* was published, apparently funded by an inheritance which had come Balius's way. This second series, four issues of which we have examined, contains nothing of interest. Balius's name appears nowhere and Pablo Ruiz is listed as the editor-in-chief. The most remarkable feature of it was that every edition contained a poster for members in the interior, inside Spain itself, to paste up on walls by way of clandestine propaganda.

Notes for Chapter 7

1. In his article "Por los fueros de la verdad," Balius has this to say: "Later came the ukase from the higher committees ordering our expulsion, but this was rejected by the rank and file in the trade union assemblies and at a plenum of FAI groups held in the Casa CNT-FAI."

2. The welcome and widespread sympathy won by the Friends of Durruti from the CNT membership are evident, not just in the powerlessness of the CNT committees and leadership to secure their expulsion, but also in the discontent and deliberation which led, following the May events, to the emergence of a conspiratorial structure within the libertarian organizations, which threw up documents entitled "Aportación a un proyecto de organización conspirativa" and "Informe respecto a la preparación de un golpe de Estado,"

as published in the anthology *Sucesos de mayo (1937)* Cuadernos de la guerra civil No. 1, (Fundación Salvador Segui, Madrid, 1987)

3. Issue No. 1 of *El Amigo del Pueblo* bears no date. The Group had distributed a notice announcing that *El Amigo del Pueblo*, the mouthpiece of the Friends of Durruti, would be appearing, on Wednesday May 19. Tavera and Ucelay mistakenly give the date of May 11, 1937, probably taken from the Manifesto reproduced on the second page of the first issue of *El Amigo del Pueblo*. Paul Sharkey gives the much more likely date of May 20. Then again, given the weekly periodicity which it was intended the paper should have, and that issue No. 2 of *El Amigo del Pueblo* was published on May 26, 1937, there can be no doubt of the date on which No. 1 appeared.

4. *Solidaridad Obrera* was under the management of Jacinto Toryho, who was appointed editor-in-chief of the CNT's main newspaper on account of his resolute defense of CNT collaborationism and discipline. He was profoundly at loggerheads with Balius, who had always been highly critical of anarcho-syndicalist collaborationism. Regarding Toryho and his enmity and friction with Balius, see the interesting study made in an otherwise deplorable article by Susana Tavera and Enric Ucelay da Cal, cited earlier: as well as Jordi Sabater's book *Anarquisme i catalanisme. La CNT i el fet naciónal catalá durant la Guerra Civil* (Ediciôns 62, Barcelona, 1986, pp. 109-110)

5. As stated by Balius in his letter to Burnett Bolloten from Cuernavaca, June 24, 1946.

6. Ibid.

7. Jordi Arquer *Història* . . . op. cit. Colonel Burillo had been involved in the arrest of Nin and the rest of the POUM leadership.

8. In fact, on June 16, four days after the date on which No. 3 of *El Amigo del Pueblo* came out, the POUM was outlawed and its militants and leaders arrested and/or murdered, in an operation, unprecedented in Spain, overseen by the CPU and Spanish Stalinists.

9. We need not, we feel, go into the differences between revolutionary marxism and Stalinism. Anyone interested in this matter can refer to issue No. 1 of *Balance*.

10. So, the Friends of Durruti did not regard the Antifascist Militias' Committee (CAMC) as dual power in embryo, but rather as a class collaboration agency. This was the same conclusion to which Nin, Azaña, Tarradellas, the Bordiguists, etc. had come and flies in the face of the academic, historiographical thesis presenting the CAMC as embryonic workers' power in contradistinction to the Generalidad.

11. In the indictment drawn up in February-March 1938 against the militants of the Bolshevik-Leninist Section, there is reference to a search carried out at the print works of one of those indicted, the printer Baldomero Palau. The

search carried out at the print works in Barcelona's Calle Salmeron uncovered a masthead for *La Voz Leninista*, used in the printing of No. 3, dated February 15, 1938. The document also mentions the discovery of two mastheads from the newspaper *El Amigo del Pueblo*. This was No. 12 of *El Amigo del Pueblo*, published in Barcelona on February 1, 1938.

Moreover, in Circular No. 4 from the Regional Labor Confederation (CNT) of Catalonia [held at the International Institute for Social history in Amsterdam], there is a reproduction of a circular issued by the Friends of Durruti (date unknown, but we imagine from August 1937) to all CNT unions in Catalonia, requesting financial assistance in the purchase of a copying machine because "it is becoming increasingly harder to get out *El Amigo del Pueblo*. Printers fight shy of agreeing to typeset and print it, on account of its clandestine status and for fear of the authorities. The day will come when we will no longer be able to get it out, because of this problem."

12. This was doubtless a printing error. The date should be August 31, 1937, since No. 8 is dated September 21 and there are only 30 days in September.

13. As he himself tells us, Balius had been jailed in May 1937: "I was held on the first gallery of the Model Prison. This was in May 1937, after the May events." [Jaime Balius "No es hora de confusionismos" in *Le Combat Syndicaliste* of April 14, 1971]. However, the first report of Balius having been jailed appeared in issue No. 4 of *El Amigo del Pueblo* dated June 22, 1937. Given that issue No. 3 of the Friends of Durruti's mouthpiece was dated June 12, 1937, the likelihood is that Balius's incarceration coincided with the mass arrests of POUM militants, launched on June 16 when the POUM was declared outside the law.

14. At no time do we enter into an examination of Durruti as a person, nor of his political ideology. We merely mention the claims of his contemporaries. It is not out of place to recall that Balius held that the Friends of Durruti Group, despite the name, had no ideological links with Durruti. Then again, Durruti was primarily an activist and was never a theorist, nor did he ever claim to be. We should point out also that *Soli* did not reprint Durruti's broadcast speeches verbatim and unabridged.

EL AMIGO DEL PUEBLO
PORTAVOZ DE LOS AMIGOS DE DURRUTI

Año 1 | Núm. 5 | 20 céntimos | Redacción y Administración: Rambla de las Flores, 1 | Teléfono 18721 | Barcelona, martes, 20 de Julio de 1937

DESPUES DE MAYO

UNA SITUACIÓN INTOLERABLE

EDITORIAL — Una teoria revolucionaria

El giro que han tomado los acontecimientos después de los sucesos de mayo es realmente aleccionador. En la correlación de las fuerzas, que se manifestaron en la calle durante las jornadas de julio, se ha producido una sensible transformación.

Aquel poderío gigantesco que giraba en torno de la C.N.T. y de la F.A.I., un año ha, ha sufrido un notable relajamiento. No se trata de que las masas obreras se hayan divorciado del sentir revolucionario que es algo inherente a la organización confederal y específica. Los trabajadores continúan abrazando el mismo frenesí de las primeras jornadas.

La trayectoria descendente ha de atribuirse exclusivamente a la ausencia de un programa concreto y de unas realizaciones inmediatas y que por este hecho hemos caído en las redes de los sectores contrarrevolucionarios en el preciso momento que las circunstancias se desenvolvían netamente favorables para una coronación de las aspiraciones del proletariado. Y al no dar libre cauce a aquel despertar de julio, en un sentido netamente de clase, hemos posibilitado un predominio pequeño-burgués que de ninguna de las maneras podía producirse si en los medios confederales y anarquistas, hubiese prevalecido una decisión unánime de asentar el proletariado en la dirección del país.

Pero no ha habido una visión de las incidencias vividas. En julio no interpretamos aquella hora grandiosa. Tuvimos miedo. Los cañones de las escuadras extranjeras infundieron pusilanimidad a un crecido porcentaje de militantes. Cedimos terreno a los sectores que más tarde se han enfrentado con las organizaciones típicamente revolucionarias con pretensiones de un destacado cariz reaccionario.

No consideramos que los fracasos hay que achacarlos exclusivamente a los individuos. Tenemos sendas pruebas de que la inmoralidad ha contribuido enormemente al desenvolvimiento de fechas atrás. Pero lo que verdaderamente ha contribuido, es decir, ha decidido la pérdida sensible de una revolución que solo se podía escapar de las manos de unos incapaces, es la omisión de una directriz que hubiera marcado de una manera inconfundible el camino a seguir.

La improvisación siempre ha dado resultados pésimos. Nuestra presunción de que las concreciones sociales se forjan sin que exista una determinante que vele celosamente por la salvaguarda de las premisas de la revolución, es un tanto desplazada. Y en julio el determinante eran la C.N.T. y la F.A.I., cometiéndose la simpleza de que una revolución de tipo social podía compartir sus latidos económicos y sociales, con los factores enemigos. Y este fué el error máximo, pues hemos dado calor a la pequeña burguesía que se ha vuelto airada contra la clase trabajadora cuando por efecto de los derroteros de la guerra ha hallado un firme sostén en las llamadas potencias democráticas.

En mayo se volvió a plantear el mismo pleito. De nuevo se ventilaba la supremacía en la dirección de la revolución. Pero los mismos individuos que en julio se atemorizaron por el peligro de una intervención extranjera, en las jornadas de mayo volvieron a incurrir en aquella falta de visión que culminó en el fatídico «Alto el fuego» que, más tarde, se tradujo, a pesar de haberse concertado una tregua en un desarme insistente y en una despiadada represión de la clase trabajadora. La causa la hemos señalado. De pruebas tenemos muchas. A los pocos días de julio, algunos militantes que han participado en las formaciones híbridas, afirmaban públicamente que se había de renunciar al comunismo libertario. Pero lo que no se puede comprender es que después de esta negación, no se presenciase inmediatamente una afirmación clara y categórica.

De manera que, al despojarnos de un programa, léase comunismo libertario, nos entregamos por entero a nuestros adversarios que poseían y poseen un programa y unas directrices. Desde este instante se perfiló nuestro desplazamiento, pues dábamos razón a los partidos que tan sañudamente habíamos combatido y a quienes entregamos en bandeja una revolución que nadie nos podía regatear. La falta de sentido de clase también ha coadyuvado a la etapa de descenso que estamos presenciando. A través de determinados discursos se han lanzado expresiones de un calibre contrarrevolucionario. Y en nuestras intervenciones hemos ido a remolque de la mesocracia, siendo así que había de ser la organización mayoritaria de julio la que había de disponer, en un sentido absoluto, de la cosa pública. Y a los partidos pequeño-burgueses había que apiadarlos en julio y en mayo. Opinamos que cualquier otro sector, en el caso de disponer de una mayoría absoluta como la que poseíamos nosotros se hubiera erigido en árbitro absoluto de la situación.

En el número anterior de nuestro portavoz proclamábamos un programa. Sentamos la necesidad de una Junta revolucionaria, de un predominio económico de los Sindicatos y de una estructuración libre de los Municipios. Nuestra Agrupación ha querido señalar una pauta por el temor de que en circunstancias similares a julio y a mayo, se proceda de una manera idéntica. Y el triunfo radica en la existencia de un programa que ha de ser respaldado, sin titubeos, por los fusiles.

No obstante el cúmulo de errores cometidos, es presumible que más tarde o más temprano se volverá a manifestar el proletariado. Pero lo que se ha de procurar es que en la ocasión inmediata no vuelvan a prevalecer los timoratos y los incapaces que nos han situado en un terreno que está erizado de sumas dificultades.

Las revoluciones sin una teoría no siguan adelante. «Los Amigos de Durruti» hemos trazado nuestro pensamiento que puede ser objeto de los retoques propios de las grandes conmociones sociales, pero que radica en dos puntos esenciales que no pueden eludirse. Un programa y fusiles.

Mantengamos el criterio apuntado en los Sindicatos, en los lugares de trabajo. Hagamos prevalecer nuestros propósitos. Sin nerviosismos estériles, sin precipitaciones contraproducentes, preparemos a la clase trabajadora para que sepa escalar de una vez el lugar que le corresponde y que por falta de una teoría revolucionaria se ha perdido lastimosamente.

HONRADEZ

No lo olvidéis, camaradas

8. Balius' Pamphlet: *Towards a Fresh Revolution*

The pamphlet *Hacia una nueva revolución*, of which fifty thousand copies were printed,[1] even though it was published clandestinely, fleshed out a program which had until then been rather vague. Balius set to work on the drafting of it sometime around November 1937,[2] and it was published by the Friends of Durruti Group in January 1938.[3] Without doubt, it is the Friends of Durruti's most extensive text and for this reason deserves a separate comment.

The pamphlet's most significant theoretical contributions had been set out before in editorials in issues Nos. 5, 6, and 7 of *El Amigo del Pueblo*, which is to say, between July 20 and August 31, 1937.

So, the pamphlet has no great theoretical novelties to offer. The great novelty of it resides in any case in the adoption by an anarchists group of concepts which marxism had systematized as the most elementary idiom of the revolutionary theory of the proletariat. On that score the vocabulary used by Balius differs from that used by the marxist classics. But as we shall see, it is not too hard to recognize a familiar idea even when it is called by different names.

The pamphlet comprised 31 pages,[4] divided into eight chapters. The first chapter offered a short historical introduction, in which Balius offered an overview of the period between the Primo de Rivera dictatorship and October 1934. In the second chapter, the events leading up to the revolutionary uprising in July 1936 were examined. A number of claims stand out, being startling, though none the less true for that:

> The people had to go and look for weapons. They took them by right of conquest. Gained them by their own exertions. They were given nothing: not by the Government of the Republic, not by the Generalidad — not one rifle.

The Friends of Durruti's searching analaysis of the revolution of July 19, 1936 is worth highlighting:

> The vast majority of the working population stood by the CNT. Inside Catalonia, the CNT was the majority organization. What happened, that the CNT did not make its revolution, the people's revolution, the revolution of the majority of the proletariat?
>
> What happened was what had to happen. The CNT was utterly devoid of revolutionary theory. We did not have a concrete program. We had no idea where we were going. We had lyricism aplenty: but when all is said and done, we did not know what to do with our masses of workers or how to give substance to the popular effusion which erupted inside our organizations. By not knowing what to do, we handed the revolution on a platter to the bourgeoisie and the marxists who support the farce of yesteryear. What is worse, we allowed the bourgeoisie a breathing space: to return, to re-form and to behave as would a conqueror.
>
> The CNT did not know how to live up to its role. It did not want to push ahead with the revolution with all of its consequences.

So, according to the Friends of Durruti, the July revolution failed because the CNT lacked a revolutionary theory and a revolutionary program. From anarchist quarters, lots of reasons have been advanced for this and several different explanations offered of the character of the July revolution: some of these arguments are pretty attractive, but neither Vernon Richards, Semprun Maura, Abad de Santillán, Garcia Oliver, nor Berneri were as plain and clear-cut, nor did they probe the nature of the July revolution as deeply as the Friends of Durruti did in the extract just cited.

Nevertheless, this is only a sampler, because the Friends of Durruti, who were not brilliant theorists nor gifted organizers, but essentially barricade fighters who argued their theoretical case from deliberation upon first hand experiences, with no more than their class instinct to guide them, arrived, in the text which we shall being looking at anon, at one of the finest contemporary analyses of the Spanish **revolution**. An analysis that deserves to be considered, and which we ought not to tag as anarchist or marxist, because it is an analysis from men who did not dice with words but with lives and primarily with their very own lives:

> When an organization's whole existence has been spent preaching revolution, it has an obligation to act whenever a favorable set of circumstances arises. And in July the occasion did present itself. The CNT ought to have leapt into the driver's seat in the country, delivering a severe *coup de grace* to all that is outmoded and archaic. In this way, we would have won the war and saved the revolution.
>
> But it did the opposite. It collaborated with the bourgeoisie in the affairs of the state, precisely when the State was crumbling away on all sides. It bolstered up Companys and company. It breathed a lungful of oxygen into an anemic, terror-stricken bourgeoisie. One of the most direct reasons why the revolution has been asphyxiated and the CNT displaced, is that it behaved like a minority group, even though it had a majority in the streets. [. . .]
>
> On the other hand, we would assert that revolutions are totalitarian, no matter who says otherwise. What happens is that the various aspects of revolution are progressively dealt with, but with the proviso that the class which represents the new order of things is the one with the most responsibility. And when things are done by halves, we have what presently concerns us, the disaster of July.
>
> In July a committee of Antifascist Militias was set up. It was not a class organ. Bourgeois and counterrevolutionary factions had their representatives on it. It looked as if this Committee had been set up as a counterbalance to the Generalidad. But it was all a sham.

First of all, we ought to underline the definition of the Central Antifascist Militias Committee as a class collaborationist agency and not as the germ of embryonic worker power. On this score, there is total agreement with Nin in the articles he wrote after the May events. And of course the Friends of Durruti were unaware of that article.

To the truism that a revolutionary organization's sole obligation is to make revolution was added a critique of the CNT's cooperation in the rescue and reconstruction of the State.

Thus far, the arguments of the Friends of Durruti were orthodoxly anarchist. But as a direct result of these arguments, or perhaps it would be better to say, as a result of the contradictions within the CNT which was embroiled in such an unlikely anarchist endeavor as rescuing and rebuilding a crumbling capitalist State, we come to a remarkable theoretical advance by the Friends of Durruti: **revolutions are totalitarian**. If such a self-evident truth was at odds with the libertarian mentality, then it has to be said that an anarchist revolution is a contradiction defying resolution. Something of the sort was experienced by the anarchists of Spain in 1936.

In its next section, Balius's pamphlet dealt with the revolutionary uprising in May 1937. The Friends of Durruti's reasoning was as plain and radical as could be: the roots of the May events went back to July **because of the failure to make the revolution in July**.

> Social revolution could have been a fact in Catalonia. [. . .] But the events took a different turn. The revolution was not made in Catalonia. Realizing that once again the proletariat was saddled with a leadership of quibblers, the petit bourgeoisie, which had gone into hiding in its back-rooms in July, hastened to join the battle.

Their analysis of Stalinism and of the crucial role it played as a springboard for counterrevolution was not only perceptive but probed further into a profile of the social strata which had afforded it support. It ought to be pointed out, though, that the term "Stalinism" was never used: instead the preferred terms were "socialism" or "marxist" though these carried the meaning with which we today invest the term "Stalinism" from all historical and ideological angles:

> In Catalonia, socialism has been a pitiful creature. Its ranks have been swollen by members opposed to revolution. They have captained the counterrevolution. It has spawned a UGT which has been turned into an appendage of the GEPCI. Marxist leaders have sung the praises of counterrevolution. They have sculpted slogans about the issue of a united front while first eliminating the POUM,[6] then trying to repeat the exercise with the CNT.
>
> The maneuvers of the petit bourgeoisie, in alliance with the socialists and communists, culminated in the events of May.

According to the Friends of Durruti, the May events represented a deliberate provocation designed to create a climate of indecision preparatory to dealing the working class a decisive blow, in order to put paid once and for all to a potentially revolutionary situation:

> The counterrevolution wanted the working class on the streets in a disorganized manner so that they might be crushed. They

> partially attained their objectives: thanks to the stupidity of some leaders who gave the cease-fire order and dubbed the 'Friends of Durruti' agents provocateurs just when the streets had been won and the enemy eliminated."

The accusation leveled against the anarchist leaders (and although no names are given, we cannot help thinking of Garcia Oliver and Federica Montseny) is not intended as an insult but is a fair assessment of their performance during the May days.

The Friends of Durruti's belief was that the counterrevolution had achieved its chief aim — Valencia government control of public order.

The Friends of Durruti's description and assessment of the workers' backlash against the Stalinist provocation, that is, the May event, is extremely interesting:

a) It was a spontaneous backlash.

b) There was no revolutionary leadership.

c) Within a few hours, the workers had scored a resounding military victory. Only a few buildings in the city center were holding out and these could have been taken with ease.

d) The Uprising had been defeated, not militarily, but politically.

> At the end of a few hours, the tide had turned in the favor of the proletarians enrolled in the CNT who, as they held in July, defended their rights with guns in hand. We took the streets. They were ours. There was no power on earth that could have wrested them from us. Working class areas fell to us quickly. Then the enemy's territory was eaten away, little by little, to a redoubt in a section of the residential district — the city center which would have fallen soon, but for the defection of the CNT committees.

Next, Balius justified the Friends of Durruti's actions during the bloody week of May 1937: the Friends of Durruti, in a context of indecision and widespread disorientation in the workers' ranks, issued a leaflet and a manifesto, in the intention of affording events a revolutionary lead and purpose. Later the Group's primary concern in the face of the CNT leadership's incredible policy of appeasement and fraternization was that the barricades should not come down unconditionally or without assurances.

According to Balius, in May there had still been time to salvage the revolution,[7] and the Friends of Durruti had been alone in showing themselves equal to the circumstances. The CNT-FAI's blinkered attitude to the repression that would needlessly batten upon the revolutionary workers had already been foretold by the Friends of Durruti.

The next chapter in the pamphlet tackles the subject of Spain's independence. The entire chapter is replete with wrong-headed notions which are short-sighted or better suited to the petit bourgeoisie. A cheap and vacuous nationalism is championed with limp, simplistic references to international politics. So we shall pass over this chapter, saying only that the Friends of Durruti subscribed to bourgeois, simplistic and/or backward-looking ideas with regard to nationalism.[8]

The chapter given over to collaborationism and class struggle is, by contrast, greatly interesting. Collaboration in the government business of the bourgeois State was the big accusation which the Group leveled at the CNT. The Friends of Durruti's criticism was even more radical than that of Berneri, because Berneri was critical of **CNT participation in the Government**, whereas the Group was critical of **the CNT's collaboration with the capitalist State**. It was not just a matter of two slightly divergent formulations, but rather of a quite different political outlook underpinning it. To return to the pamphlet:

> There must be no collaboration with capitalism, whether outside the bourgeois state or from within government itself. As producers, our place is in the unions, reinforcing the only bodies that ought to survive a revolution headed by the workers. [. . .] And the State cannot be retained in the face of the Unions — let alone bolstered up by our own forces. The fight against capitalism goes on. Inside our own territory, there is still a bourgeoisie connected to the international bourgeoisie. The problem is now what it has been for years.

The Friends of Durruti ventured to suggest that the collaborationists were allied with the bourgeoisie, which was tantamount to saying that the anarchist ministers and all who advocated collaborationism **were allied with the bourgeoisie.**

> The collaborationists are allies of the bourgeoisie. Individuals who advocate such relations have no feeling for the class struggle, nor have they the slightest regard for the unions. Never must we accept the consolidation of our enemy's positions. The enemy must be beaten. [. . .] There can be absolutely no common ground between exploiters and exploited. Which shall prevail, only battle can decide. Bourgeois or workers. Certainly not both of them at once.

However, the Group at no time took the next definitive step, the inevitable break with **a collaborationist type organization** which had demonstrated its **inability to call off and finish with this policy of alliance with the bourgeoisie.** The Group never proposed a break with the CNT, and the denunciation of that organization as one of capitalism's organizations. The ideological premises set out were not explored in all that they entailed. It was easier to point the accusing finger at a few individuals, a few leaders who advocated a policy of collaboration with the bourgeoisie than to arrive at the stark and dismal conclusion that the CNT was an organization for collaborating with the bourgeoisie, by virtue of its very nature as a trade union. **It was not the anarchist ministers who were leading the CNT away from its principles, but rather the CNT that was churning out ministers.** But the Group reckoned that the trade unions were class struggle organizations. Even the Catalan UGT, Stalinist through and through and nothing more than an instrument of the PSUC, the party of counterrevolution, was not regarded as an organ of the bourgeoisie. So it was impossible for the Friends of Durruti to take that crucial step. If they could not acknowledge the true nature of the unions[9] as capitalist State machinery, they could not contemplate breaking with the CNT either. Very much the opposite; the unions were a fundamental factor in the Group's theoretical argument. **Its charges were leveled at individuals, not at organizations.** There was no acknowledgment of the **disease**, nor of its causes: only a few of the symptoms were recognized.[10]

The pamphlet continues with an exposition of the positions and program of the Friends of Durruti. Perhaps because they were hastily drafted, or because of the poor reception awaiting them at that point, the main and most typical tactical political positions, were set out in a more incomplete, confused and vague form than in previous expositions. Those points were as follows: 1. Workers' direction of the war through a workers' revolutionary army. 2. Rejection of class collaboration, meaning that the unions were to be strengthened. 3. Socialization of the economy. 4. Anticlericalism. 5. Socialization of distribution, through eradication of bureaucracy and universal rationing of all consumer products. 6. Equal pay. 7. Popular courts. 8. Equality between countryside and town, and defense of the agrarian collectivizations. 9. Worker control of public order.

The central basis of the program was the July experience, which the Friends of Durruti very tellingly depicted as a successful uprising, which had been found wanting in revolutionary theory and revolutionary objectives:

> They had no idea which course of action to pursue. There was no theory. Year after year we had spent speculating around ab-

> stractions. What is to be done? the leaders were asking themselves then. And they allowed the revolution to be lost. Such exalted moments leave no time for hesitancy. Rather, one has to know where one is going. This is precisely the vacuum we seek to fill, since we feel that what happened in July and May must never happen again.
>
> We are introducing a slight variation in anarchism into our program. The establishment of a Revolutionary Junta.

The revolutionary Junta was described by the Group as a vanguard established for the purpose of repressing the revolution's enemies:

> As we see it, the revolution needs organisms to oversee it and to repress, in an organized sense, hostile sectors. As current events have shown, such sectors do not accept oblivion unless they are crushed.
>
> There may be anarchist comrades who feel certain ideological misgivings, but the lesson of experience is enough to induce us to stop pussy-footing.
>
> Unless we want a repetition of what is happening with the present revolution, we must proceed with the utmost energy against those who are not identified with the working class.

After this preamble, the Friends of Durruti set out their revolutionary program, which boiled down to three major points: 1. Establishment of a **Revolutionary Junta** or National Defense Council, the task of which would be to oversee the war, control public order and handle international affairs and revolutionary propaganda. 2. **All economic power to the unions**: this meant the formation of an outright trade union capitalism. 3. **Free Municipality** as the basic cell of territorial organization, the intersection between State decentralization and the quintessentially anarchist federal approach.

The pamphlet closed with a final section bearing the same title as the whole pamphlet: there was a realistic, categorical statement: "the revolution no longer exists." After a long string of speculations and questions about the immediate prospect, acknowledging the strength of the counterrevolution, a timid, utopian, well-meaning and perhaps rhetorical summons was issued to a future anarchist revolution capable of satisfying human aspirations and the anarchist ideal. However, the counterrevolution's success in the republican zone and the fascists' victory in the war were by then inevitable, as Balius conceded in his 1978 foreword ("Forty Years Ago") to an English-language edition of *Hacia una nueva revolución* (*Towards a Fresh Revolution*).

Notes to Chapter 8

1. According to Arquer, op. cit., although the figure seems to us a bit inflated, if not incredible.
2. On page 16 of the pamphlet *Hacia una nueva revolución* it is stated: "Sixteen months have past. What remains? Of the spirit or July, only a memory. Of the organisms of July, a yesterday." From which our deduction is that the pamphlet was drafted around November 1937, which is to say, sixteen months after July 1936.
3. In his 1978 introduction to the English-language edition of the pamphlet, *Towards a Fresh Revolution,* he says that it was published [he says "written" when he ought to have said "published"] in mid-1938: and he also explains the background to its publication:

> "I shall now proceed with a short introduction to our pamphlet: *Hacia una nueva revolución*. First of all, when was it written? Around mid-1938. [. . .] Such was the tragic hour when we of the Friends of Durruti, at the Group's last session, after prolonged examination of the disaster into which the counterrevolution had plunged us, and regardless of the scale of the disaster, refused to accept the finality of such defeat. The infamous policy pursued by Largo Caballero, whose government contained several anarchist militants, had eroded the revolutionary morale of the rearguard: and the Negrin government, the government of defeat and capitulation, gave the defeat hecatomb proportions. For this reason we decided to publish *Hacia una nueva revolución* which was, as we said, a message of hope and a determination to renew the fight against an international capitalism which had mobilized its gendarmes of the 1930s (in other words, its blackshirts and its brownshirts) to put down the Spanish working class at whose head marched the anarchists and the revolutionary rank and file of the CNT.

See the Friends of Durruti Group *Towards a Fresh Revolution* (New Anarchist Library (2) Translated by Paul Sharkey. Sanday, Orkney 1978).
However, in spite of what Balius claims in no. 12 of *El Amigo del Pueblo* there was a reference to the pamphlet, *recently published* by the Group and entitled *Towards a Fresh Revolution*. Since issue No. 12 of the Friends of Durruti's mouthpiece is dated February 1, 1938, it can be stated that the pamphlet appeared in January 1938.
4. We have consulted the pamphlet in the original, which differs slightly from the reprint by Etcétera, which is only 28 pages in length, although the text is full and complete.

5. Published in No. 2 of *Balance* serie de estudios e investigaciones, Barcelona, 1994.
6. Note the distinction drawn by the Friends of Durruti between the "marxist" leaders (marxist meaning Stalinist counterrevolutionaries) and the exclusion of the POUM (POUMists as revolutionaries different from the Stalinists) from the united front.
7. In 1971 Balius reiterated this view: "And I want to finish with the uprising of May 1937. The mistakes made could still have been set right. Again we had mastery of the streets. Two front-line divisions made for Barcelona, but the 'cease-fire' and the pressures and arguments brought to bear upon the commanders of the two divisions [the CNT's Rojinegra division commanded by Maximo Franco (a Group member) and the POUM division under Josep Rovira: they were stopped thanks to the overtures by the CNT member Molina and the Defense councilor, the CNT's Isgleas prevented them from reaching the Catalan capital. The counterrevolution's day had come. The hesitancy in May did for the 20th century's proletarian epic.
Had we been able to call upon a capable revolutionary leadership, we would have made and consolidated a revolution that might have set an example for the world and would have put paid once and for all to the shabby Muscovite bogey" (Jaime Balius "Recordando julio de 1936" in *Le Combat syndicaliste* of April 1, 1971).
8. And yet Balius had (in 1935?) published through the Editorial Renacer a pamphlet entitled *El nacionalismo y el proletariado* in which he set out, from an anarchist and workerist angle, very intriguing ideas on the matter of nationalism.
9. See Benjamin Peret and G. Munis *Los sindicatos contra la revolución* (FOR, Apartado 5355, Barcelona, 1992). See also the appeal issued by the Bolshevik-Leninist Section of Spain on June 26, 1937 (ten days after the outlawing of the POUM) to the POUM left:

> Instead of using a United Front to marshal the revolutionary anarchist masses against their anarcho-reformist leaders, your leadership blindly followed the CNT. This fact was most plainly demonstrated during the May events, when the POUM ordered a retreat before any concrete objective, such as the disarming of the security forces, had been achieved. During the events, the POUM was merely an appendage of the anarcho-reformist leadership.
>
> The reverse side of this policy of support for the CNT bureaucracy has been the abandonment of the committees of workers, peasants and combatants which had sprung up spontaneously. So you are cut off from the masses. Your leaders concocted new theories under which the unions, those aged bureaucratic ma-

> chines, could take power. You had done nothing to halt the dissolution of the local committees, while you were expelling our comrades for carrying out propaganda on the committees' behalf. But during the May events you swiftly turned to the defense committees. This eleventh hour stance was of course utterly inadequate, for it is not enough to issue a hasty call for "committees": they have to be organized in practical terms. But in fact, right after the May events your platonic solicitude for the committees ceased completely.

(Bolshevik-Leninist Section of Spain — (on behalf of the Fourth International) "El viejo POUM ha muerto: viva el POUM de la IV Internaciónal," Barcelona June 26, 1937)

10. In 1939 Eduardo Maurico came up with a very similar critique of the Friends of Durruti's program:

> For such groups [groups such as the Friends of Durruti] the root of all evil had been the abandonment of 'principles' by the leadership. A reversion to 'wholesome principles', a return to 'purity', 'a fresh start' — that in its entirety was the program and the rallying cry of these factions. Now, starting afresh is an utter impossibility. There is more likely to be a reenactment of history. There can be no return to the situation prior to July 19: but the same mistakes can be made in similar circumstances. The biggest mistake that these factions today can make is to fail to draw all of the lessons evident in the Spanish Revolution, all in the name of 'purity of principles.' That initial mistake would induce them sooner or later to make the same mistakes and compromises which today they are against. And the primary consequence of the Spanish Revolution is that the compromises by the Garcia Olivers and the Cipriano Meras were not due to the abandonment of the CNT's traditional 'apoliticism,' but were down to that 'apoliticism' itself, that is, to the lack of **a revolutionary theory, in the absence of which revolution is impossible.** (Lenin)

[O. Emem "Situación revoluciónaria. El poder. El partido." in ¡Experience española. Faits et documents No. 2, Paris, August 1939]

9. Balius's Thoughts from Exile in 1939

An exiled Balius had two articles printed in the French anarchist review *L'Espagne nouvelle.* The first of these marked the third anniversary of July 19, 1936. The second, published in September 1939, by which time France and England had formally declared war on Germany, was devoted to May 1937. Both articles were the result of long, considered reflection by Balius, who signed both articles in his capacity as "secretary of the Friends of Durruti."

Both these articles stand out on account of the precision of the language used and of their central focus upon the fundamental issues raised by the Spanish revolution. Thus, they offer us with the utmost clarity of Balius's thinking on the question of power, the indispensable function of a revolutionary leadership and the need to destroy the State and introduce a new structure in its place (in earlier writings, this was described as a revolutionary junta) capable of repressing counterrevolutionary forces.

In the article entitled "July 1936: import and possibilities" he contradicted those who argued that the July events were simply the result of the struggle against the rising by the military and the fascists, which is to say that "without the army rebellion there would have been no armed popular movement." Instead, Balius claimed that this outlook was in keeping with Popular Front-ism, the result of the subordination of the working class to the republican bourgeoisie, itself the chief reason why the proletariat had been defeated. Balius recalled how the republican bourgeoisie had refused the workers the arms with which to confront the fascist rebellion:

> In Barcelona itself, we had to suffer the Transport Union to be stormed by Generalidad goons who, only hours before the crucial battle, were still eager to take away the rifles which we had seized from aboard the Manuel Arnús, and which were intended for use against the fascists.

According to Balius, the victory over the military had only been achieved in those places where the workers, weapons at the ready, and with no sort of deals with the petit bourgeoisie, had taken on the fascists. Wheresoever the workers — as in Zaragoza — had hesitated or made deals, the victory had gone to the fascists.

The most important issued raised in July 1936, according to Balius, was not the army's success in a few areas in Spain. The most important issue had arisen inside the republican zone: who took power and who directed the war? To which question there could be only two answers: the republican bourgeoisie, or the proletariat:

> But the most important issue arose in our zone. It was a matter of determining who had won. Was it the workers? In which case the governance of the country fell to us. But . . . the petit bourgeoisie as well? That was the mistake.

Balius argued that the working class ought to have taken power regardless in July 1936. Which would have represented the only guarantee and only chance of victory in the war:

> "The CNT and the FAI which were the soul of the movement in Catalonia could have afforded the July events their proper color. Who could have stopped them? Instead of which, we allowed the Communist Party (PSUC) to rally the opportunists, the bourgeois right, etc., . . . on the terrain of the counterrevolution.
>
> In such times, it is up to one organization to take the lead. Only one could have: **ours**.
>
> [. . .] Had the workers known how to act as masters in antifascist Spain, the war would have been won, and the revolution would not have had to endure so many deviations right from the start. We could have had the victory. But what we managed to gain with four handguns, we lost when we had whole arse-

nals full of arms. For those culpable for the defeat, we have to look past Stalinism's hired assassins, past the thieves like Prieto, past scum like Negrin and past the usual reformists: **we bore the guilt** for not having it in us to do away with all this riffraff [. . .] But, while we are all jointly to blame, there are those who bear a particularly heavy burden of responsibility. Namely, the leaders of the CNT-FAI, whose reformist approach in July and whose counterrevolutionary intervention in May 1937 especially barred the way to the working class and dealt the revolution a mortal blow.

Such was Balius's summing-up of the thousand doubts and objections which the anarcho-syndicalist leaders had faced in July 1936, regarding the minority status of the anarchist presence outside of Catalonia, the need to maintain antifascist unity and the repeated compromises which the war forced upon the revolution. Balius claimed that the anarchists' victory in Catalonia could have presaged the quick crushing of the fascist uprising all across Spain, **had the proletariat taken power**. According to Balius, **that was the mistake made in July 1936: power had not been taken**. And out of that mistake came the rapid degeneration of the revolution, and its difficulties. That mistake left the door open for the growth of the counterrevolution, of which Stalinism was the chief architect. But Balius reckoned the blame lay, not with the Stalinists and the republican bourgeoisie, but rather with those anarchist leaders who had preferred antifascist unity — which is to say, collaboration with the bourgeoisie, the State and capitalist institutions — over proletarian revolution.

In his article on the events of May 1937, published in September 1939, and entitled "May 1937: a historical date for the proletariat," Balius described the two years following May 1937 as the simple aftermath of those revolutionary events. According to Balius, May 1937 was not a protest, but rather a consciously revolutionary uprising of the Catalan proletariat, which **succeeded militarily and failed politically**.

The failure was down to treachery by the anarchist leaders. Again we find the charge of treason leveled by the Friends of Durruti during the events of May 1937, only to be retracted later in *El Amigo del Pueblo:*

But the treason of the reformist wing of the CNT-FAI manifested itself here.

Repeating the dereliction shown in the July events, again they sided with the bourgeois democrats. They issued the cease-fire order. The proletariat was reluctant to abide by that call and in

> a raging fury, ignoring the orders from its faint-hearted leaders, it carried on defending its positions.

And this is how Balius depicted the role played by the Friends of Durruti in May 1937:

> We, the Friends of Durruti, who fought in the front lines, sought to ward off the disaster which would have been the people's constant fare, had they laid down their arms. We issued the call for the fighting to be resumed and that the fighting should not cease without certain conditions first having been met. Unfortunately, the spirit of attack had already been broken and the fighting was halted without its revolutionary objectives having been achieved.

Balius very vividly underlined the paradox of the proletariat's having succeeded militarily but failed politically:

> This was the first time in the entire history of social struggles that the victors surrendered to the vanquished. And without even the slightest assurance that the vanguard of the proletariat would not be touched, dismantling of the barricades began: the city of Barcelona returned to its appearance of normality, as if nothing had happened.

In Balius's analysis, the May events appeared as a crossroads: either the revolution was forsworn once and for all, or power was taken. And he explained away the anarchists' constant retreat since July as the fruits of the damnable Popular Front-ist policy of alliance with the republican bourgeoisie. And also as a consequence of the divorce existing within the CNT between a counterrevolutionary leadership and a revolutionary rank and file. May 1937 was a failure **because the workers failed to come up with a revolutionary leadership**:

> "The proletariat was at a fatal crossroads. There were only two courses to choose between: either bend the knee before the counterrevolution or prepare to impose one's own power, to wit, **proletarian power.**
>
> The drama of the Spanish working class is characterized by the most absolute divorce existing between the grassroots and the leadership. The leadership was always counterrevolutionary. By contrast, the Spanish workers [. . .] have always stood head and shoulders above their leaders when it comes to perceiving events

> and to interpretation of them. Had those heroic workers found a revolutionary leadership, they would have written one of the most important pages in their history while the whole world looked on."

According to Balius, in May 1937, the Catalan proletariat **had urged the CNT to take power**:

> For the essence of the May Events, one must look to the proletariat's unshakable determination to place a workers' leadership in charge of the armed struggle, the economy, and the entire existence of the country. Which is to say (for any anarchist not afraid of the words) that the proletariat was fighting for **the taking of power** which would have come to pass through the destruction of the old bourgeois instruments and the erection in their place, of a new structure based upon the committees that surfaced in July, only to be promptly suppressed by the reaction and the reformists."

In these two articles, Balius had broached the fundamental point of the revolution and Spanish civil war, without which what happened remains incomprehensible: the issue of power. And he indicated too the organs which were to have embodied that power, and above all recognized the need to dismantle the capitalist State apparatus in order to erect a proletarian replacement in its place. Moreover, Balius pointed to the absence of a revolutionary leadership as having been the root cause of the Spanish revolution's failure.

After a reading of these two articles, it has to be acknowledged that the evolution of Balius's political thinking, rooted in analysis of the wealth of experience garnered during the civil war, had led him to confront issues taboo in the anarchist ideology: 1. the need for the proletariat to take power. 2. the ineluctability of the destruction of the capitalist State apparatus to clear the way for a proletarian replacement. 3. the indispensable role of a revolutionary leadership.

What we have just said does not exclude the fact that there were other facets to Balius's thinking, secondary facets, maybe, not at issue in these articles and which are in keeping with the traditional anarcho-syndicalist ideology: 1. trade union direction of the economy. 2. committees as the organs of proletarian power. 3. municipalization of the administration, etc.

There cannot be any doubt that Balius, operating on the basis of the ideology of Spanish anarcho-syndicalism, had made tremendous efforts to digest the brutal experiences of civil war and the Spanish revolution. The merit of the Group lies precisely in that effort to comprehend reality and assimilate the first-hand experiences of the Spanish proletariat. Life was easier as an anarchist minister than as an anarchist revolutionary. It was easier to forswear ideology as such, that is, to renounce principles "temporarily" in the moment of truth, in order to revert to them once defeat and the passage of history had rendered contradictions irrelevant. It was easier to call for antifascist unity and a share in the governance of a capitalist State, and to embrace militarization in order to defer to a war directed by the republican bourgeoisie: than to confront those contradictions and assert that the CNT should have taken power, that the war was winnable only if the proletariat was in the driving seat, that the capitalist State had to be destroyed, and above all that the proletariat had to erect power structures of its own, use force to crush the counterrevolution and that all of this was impracticable in the absence of a revolutionary leadership. **Whether or not these conclusions were anarchist mattered a lot to those who never paused to question whether it was anarchist to prop up the capitalist State.** Between 1936 and 1939, the anarcho-syndicalist ideology was repeatedly put to the severest tests, with regards to its capability, coherence and validity. Balius's thinking, and that of the Friends of Durruti Group was the only worthwhile attempt by a Spanish anarchist group to resolve the contradictions and dereliction of principle which characterized the CNT and the FAI. If the theoretical endeavors of Balius and the Group led them to embrace conclusions that can be described as alien to anarcho-syndicalism, maybe it would be necessary to recognize anarchism's inadequacy as a revolutionary theory of the proletariat. Balius and the Group never took that step, and at all times regarded themselves as anarchists, although they stuck by their criticisms of the CNT's collaboration in the State.

We will not venture to describe such a stance as either coherent or contradictory. The Stalinist repression that battened upon revolutionaries following the May events did not target the Group as such, in that it was never outlawed, but targeted all CNT militants in general. Doubtless that helped preclude further theoretical clarification and an organizational rupture, which we, in any case, do not believe would have come to pass.

However, we concede that our analysis is overly political, subtle, inconvenient and problematical: it is much more convenient, whimsical, academic and suited to the anecdotes and caricatures on offer to fall back upon the *deus ex machina* of entryism and Trotskyist influences upon Balius and the Friends of Durruti.

10. The Friends of Durruti's Relations with the Trotskyists[1]

It requires only a cursory perusal of *El Amigo del Pueblo* or Balius's statements to establish that the Friends of Durruti were never marxists, nor influenced at all by the Trotskyists or the Bolshevik Leninist Section. But there is a school of historians determined to maintain the opposite and hence the necessity for this chapter.

For a start, we have to demolish one massive red herring: the so-called "Communist Union Manifesto" supposedly jointly endorsed by the Friends of Durruti, the POUM and the Libertarian Youth: but which, in point of fact, never existed. Its existence is just a fantasy of the historian's trade. Like Peter Pan's shadow, the "Communist Union Manifesto" acquired a life of its own and refuses to be tied to its master's slippers.

The misconstrued document in question was a "Manifesto" from Union Communiste, a French Trotskyist group which distributed it in Paris in June 1937 at a rally organized by French anarchists in the Vel d'Hiver in Paris, a rally with the participation of Federica Montseny and Garcia Oliver.[2] The initial peddler of this mistake, which was subsequently repeated by many others, was César M. Lorenzo.

As for the matter of Moulin's* sway over the Friends of Durruti, we are forced to conclude that this is an utterly unwarranted historiographical

---

*Moulin was a Pole — "a fanatical supporter of the Fourth International, and a Bolshevik through and through, as he himself admitted..."— who had

invention. From the Thalmanns' book it emerges that it was more a question of Moulin's having been swayed by the Friends of Durruti.[3] But even if this were not the case, the influence of Moulin within the Group's ideology, as set out in its leaflets, manifestoes and above all in the columns of *El Amigo del Pueblo*, does not warrant any claim that it amounted to anything of significance, if indeed it existed.

At all times the Group articulated an anarcho-syndicalist ideology, although it also voiced radical criticism of the CNT and FAI leadership. But it is a huge leap from that to claiming that the Group espoused marxist positions. In any case, we have no problem agreeing that analysis of the reality and of the uprisings in July and May led the Friends of Durruti to espouse two fundamental notions which can scarcely be described as essentially marxist — though they are that, too — so much as the most elementary idioms of any proletariat-driven revolutionary uprising.[4] Those two notions are, to borrow the Durruti-ists expressions, are as follows:

1. That one must impose a **revolutionary program**, libertarian communism, **which must be defended by force of arms**. The CNT, which had a majority on the streets, ought to have introduced libertarian communism and then should have defended it with force. In other words, which is to say, switching now to the marxist terminology: the dictatorship of the proletariat ought to have been installed.
2. There is a need for the **establishment of a Revolutionary Junta**, made up of revolutionaries who have taken part in the proletarian uprising, **to exercise power and use violence to repress the non-proletarian factions**, in order to preclude the latter's taking power, or embarking upon a counterrevolutionary process to defeat and crush the proletariat. That this Revolutionary Junta, as the Friends of Durruti call it, while others call it the vanguard or the revolutionary party, can shock only those who are shocked by words rather than by the defeat of the proletariat.

So, it seems obvious that there was an evolution within anarchist thought processes, leading the Friends of Durruti Group to embrace two

---

travelled to Spain in 1936 and joined the POUM. "After weeks spent in futile discussions with the Trotskyist group that was split into several factions and sub-factions, he had decided to pull out of it. Faced with the realities of war, particularly with the theory and practice of the FAI and the CNT (something very novel to him), he focused all his activities upon those anarchist circles at odds with the formal leadership." Quotes from the forthcoming AK Press book *Combats pour la liberté* by Pavel and Clara Thalmann.

notions fundamental to every proletarian revolutionary process and which have, of course, long since been incorporated into the elements of revolutionary marxism. But it is a very different thing to argue that the Friends of Durruti were influenced from without by Trotskyists and turned, overnight, into marxists. Such a contention has validity only as an insult in the propaganda deployed by the CNT against the Friends of Durruti.

That the Friends of Durruti were not in any way **beholden** to Spanish Trotskyists is transparent from several documents, which we shall now analyze:

a. On a number-of occasions, Balius's own statements roundly denied that the Friends of Durruti had been influenced in any way by the POUM or the Trotskyists,[5] and maintained that he still considered himself an anarchist militant, although, naturally, one very critical of the CNT's governmental and ministerial collaboration:[6]

> Anarchists may go to jail and perish as Obregón, Ascaso, Sabater, Buenaventura and Peiró have, whose lives are worthy of the praises of a Plutarch. We may die in exile, in concentration camps, in the maquis or in the death-ward, but assume ministerial positions? That is unthinkable.

b. The appeal issued by the Bolshevik-Leninist Section of Spain on June 26, 1937 (ten days after the POUM was outlawed) to the POUM's left:

> Although you do not see eye to eye with us upon every question and indeed are against our entry, you nonetheless did not have any right to reject collaboration with genuinely revolutionary groups. On the contrary: you have a duty to invite the 'Friends of Durruti', as well as ourselves, to seek some common accord on the requisite practical steps which may afford an escape from this situation and pave the way for new struggles that will lead us on to victory.

This invitation, issued by the Trotskyist group to the left of the POUM, to summon a meeting between the outlawed and persecuted POUM, the Friends of Durruti and the Bolshevik-Leninist Section of Spain, that is, between the three revolutionary groups in existence after the May events, indicates that the Friends of Durruti were deemed to be **an independent group** organizationally and ideologically, on a par with the POUM or the Bolshevik-Leninist Section of Spain:

c. This was the reaction to No. 2 of *La Voz Leninista*[7] to rejection of the invitations the Trotskyists has issued to hold a meeting between the POUM[8] left, the Friends of Durruti and the Bolshevik-Leninist Section and endorse a common manifesto:

> The 'Friends of Durruti' and the POUM's left wing have rejected a specific proposition. Following the dissolution of the POUM and the arrest of its militants, the Bolshevik-Leninist Section of Spain sent a letter to the 'Friends of Durruti', to the party's Madrid branch committee and to the left fraction in Barcelona, proposing that we jointly sign a manifesto demanding the immediate release of those arrested, the restoration of premises, uncensored freedom for the worker press, the disarming of the Assault Guards, legalization of the Control Patrols under the direction of workers' committees and a proposal for a CNT-FAI-POUM united front to press for these points.
>
> In the same letter, whose contents we may not reveal because of the police, our Committee arranged a rendezvous for discussion of any items upon which there might be differences of opinion. None of those invited showed up for the meeting nor has any thus far replied to our message. Unofficially, we have discovered that the POUM leftists did not think the time was right for a break with their E.[xecutive] C.[ommittee] and the 'Friends of Durruti' see little advantage to their aims in alliance with the Bolshevik-Leninists.
>
> In reality, the occasion could not have been better suited for the POUM's left wing and anarchism's leftist wing to demonstrate their capabilities as leaders and their resolution in difficult times.
>
> Regrettably, they have chosen to support their respective organizations' inertia rather than appear to be active alongside Trotskyists. We cannot disguise the fact that we regard this as reminiscent of the universal terror of Trotskyism.

This text, which we reproduce in its entirety, is a sufficiently clear indication to us that whereas there were strenuous efforts made on the part of the Trotskyist group led by Munis to bring influence to bear on the Friends of Durruti and on the POUM's left, that influence never amounted to anything more than a failed effort.

d. E. Wolf's report to Trotsky, dated July 6, 1937, states as follows [translated from the French original]:[9]

> A tactical switch is required at this point. In the past we focused almost exclusively on the POUM. The anarchist revolutionary workers were unduly neglected, with the exception of the Friends of Durruti. But the latter are rather few in number and it will be impossible to achieve any collaboration with them. We

even invited them, along with the left fraction of the POUM, to take part in a meeting to discuss joint action. Neither the POUMists nor the Friends would agree to the meeting. Not just because we appeared too weak to them, but because they are still under the influence of the monstrous campaign against Trotskyism. Assuredly they say to themselves: 'Why should we run such a risk and provide our enemies with further ammunition about our being "Trotskyists"?'

e. Munis's report to Trotsky, dated August 17, 1939,[10] which appears to contradict our claims regarding the Trotskyists' influence over the Group, has this to say:

> In the socialist and anarchist sectors, there is considerable scope for our work. The chief leader of the 'Friends of Durruti', ostensibly influenced by us, is espousing an outlook with quite pronouncedly marxist features. At our direct instigation, and on behalf of the 'Friends of Durruti', an initial bulletin was drafted, the text of which is still in our possession, in which the need to overhaul all anarchist theories is posited. [. . .] But we have lost ground in this regard, because of our being materially powerless to afford effective economic assistance to the 'Friends of Durruti' It is not our aim to encourage movement in our direction through financial means alone, but rather to utilize the latter to bring Bolshevik ideas to the workers who follow said current (. . .) we entertain no wild expectations, but economic resources will quickly secure us a preponderant influence that would bring the 'Friends of Durruti', partly at any rate, into the Fourth International.

Munis's painstaking report talks throughout about the prospects of influencing the Friends of Durruti ideologically and even of drawing them into the Fourth International: but that very same prospect, which **existed in August 1939**, is confirmation that it had come to nothing in 1937.

f. In the interview published by *La Lutte ouvrière,* in its editions dated February 24 and March 3, 1939, Munis took this line with regard to the Friends of Durruti:

> This circle of revolutionary workers [the Friends of Durruti] represented a beginning of anarchism's evolving in the direction of marxism. They had been driven to replace the theory of libertarian communism with that of the 'revolutionary junta' (soviet) as the embodiment of proletarian power, democratically elected by the workers. To begin with, especially after the May events,

during which the Friends of Durruti lined up with the Bolshevik-Leninists in the front line of the barricades, this group's influence made deep inroads into the (CNT) trade union center and into the 'political' group which directed it, the FAI. The panicking bureaucrats tried to take steps against the Friends of Durruti leaders, accusing them of being 'marxists' and 'politicals.' The CNT and FAI leadership passed a resolution to expel. But the Unions steadfastly refused to implement that resolution.

Unfortunately, the leaders of the Friends of Durruti have failed to capitalize upon the potential force at their disposal. In the face of charges that they are 'marxist politicals', they retreated without a fight.

[Question] Are there actual indications of the workers' turning away from the anarchist outlook and moving towards the notion of conscious proletarian power?

The anarchist leaders' collaboration with the bourgeoisie and the overall experience of the revolution and the war opened most anarchist workers' eyes to the fact that a proletarian power was vital for the protection of the revolution and of proletarian gains. Agreement between the Bolshevik vanguard and individual workers was readily achieved. But the organizational expression of that agreement failed to crystallize, partly on account of the absence of a strong Bolshevik nucleus, partly due to the absence of political clear-sightedness in the Friends of Durruti.

But I have had occasion to talk with old anarchist militants, some of them quite influential. All of them openly express the same notion: 'I can no longer stand by the ideas I supported before the war. Let me proclaim my agreement with dictatorship of the proletariat, which cannot be a party dictatorship as in the USSR, but rather that of a class. In the organs of proletarian power, all of the working class's organizations may come together and collaborate.

This intriguing and impassioned interview with Munis in *La Lutte ouvrière* merely bears out what we have been saying about the Friends of Durruti. In the first place, that they were not marxists, and secondly, that the emergence of the Friends of Durruti as a theoretical anarchist dissidence was due to the insufferable contradictions which the hard reality of war and revolution created within a Spanish anarchist movement characterized by its mammoth organizational strength and absolute theoretical vacuousness.

Let us, therefore, rehearse the historical context of dealings between the Friends of Durruti and the Bolshevik-Leninist Section of Spain. There had been contacts prior to May 1937, through the person of Moulin. It cannot strictly be claimed that Moulin exercised any ideological influence of any sort over Balius and the Group. During the May events there was no collaboration between them either. They merely encountered one another on the streets and both groups issued leaflets with watchwords calling for the fight to be continued.[11] But neither of them was strong enough to unseat the CNT leadership.

After May 1937, neither the POUM's left[12] (Josep Rebull) nor the Friends of Durruti[13] (Jaime Balius) agreed to attend a meeting summoned by the Trotskyists for the purpose of working out concerted action, as noted in *No. 2* of *La Voz Leninista* and in Wolf's report to Trotsky, dated July 6, 1937.

Only in French exile and from 1939 on was there any mention of possible Trotskyist **influence** over the Friends of Durruti, influence which, in fact, failed to prosper, as confirmed in Munis's extremely optimistic letter to Trotsky on April 27, 1940.[14]

Consequentially, no group wielded discernible influence over the Friends of Durruti. This contention, which we have attempted to demonstrate, is, we believe, how the historical record stands at present. But it is equally certain that the insults tossed around by the CNT did not fall on deaf ears, and that in the eyes of the majority of CNT militants the Friends of Durruti as a group was "suspected" of marxism, and that Friends of Durruti militants were always described as being authoritarian and/or 'marxist" in outlook. Take, for instance the claims made by Peirats who was, let it not be forgotten, chief editor of *Acracia* and one of the listed contributors to *Ideas*. Peirats was a CNT militant highly critical of collaboration with the State and was actively and prominently involved in the CNT opposition to the CNT leadership cadres' acceptance of ministerial portfolios. By November 1937, he was persuaded that the revolution had been lost and opted, despite his anti-militarist convictions, to go to the front "to seek death," by way of a sort of suicide arrangement, on account of the CNT's contradictions. However Peirats was not a sympathizer with the Friends of Durruti and in an oral[15] interview in 1976 he had this to say:

> **Question**: Were you aware of the creation and intentions of the 'Friends of Durruti' group? Were you in touch with them?
>
> **Peirats**: This was a group that emerged at the time of the May events. In fact its origins, I believe, can be traced back to the autumn of 1936, when the campaign for militarization started. There were lots of comrades at that time unwilling to militarize and they quit the fronts.

Question: Prior to Durruti's death?

Peirats: Yes, before Durruti's death, but especially afterwards, there were lots of comrades who refused to be militarized. The Durruti Column was still a Militias unit, not yet the 26th Division. Quite a few defied instructions and returned to the rearguard, creating a certain climate there. These were the ones that fought during the May events in Barcelona, and although there were other fighters as well, it was they who bore the brunt of the attack. When things ended in such a disgraceful compromise, there was a few who hoisted the rebel flag again, formed the "Friends of Durruti" group, brought out the newspaper *El Amigo del Pueblo* and kept in touch. But they had little impact, for some of them were not genuinely anarchists: they were merely revolutionaries and this created a certain malaise. They were not widely welcomed, even in quarters that we might term refractory towards the Organization's watchwords. I am merely articulating my feelings here. As I knew the individuals concerned, I never had any real sympathy with the 'Friends of Durruti', because I found its leanings very authoritarian. Talk along the lines of "We are going to impose this, and whoever does not . . . we will shoot him" struck me as rather Bolshevistic. And for that reason I was not a follower of theirs. I did attend some meetings, but always for discussions with them. The attitudes displayed by some of them ensured that many of us held back from helping them. And they achieved nothing. They themselves devalued their own work. The real work of opposition, therefore, carried on outside of them [. . .] In the end, around about October 1937, I felt so weary, because of the creeping counterrevolution everywhere, and I struck a heroic or suicidal pose, saying to myself: "Let death come if it will, but I am off to the front." Off I went as a volunteer, and from then on I took no further interest in the rearguard.

Peirats's testimony offers us the key to anarcho-syndicalist rationale and psychology. The Friends of Durruti, according to Peirats, were authoritarians and Bolshevistic, and that was reason enough to have no truck with them and even to go to the extreme of embracing militarism and espousing a suicidal, passive attitude to the progress of the bourgeois counterrevolution. Peirats, who, while in exile, took upon himself the CNT's commission to write an official history[16] of the CNT during the civil war, could not accept that there is nothing more authoritarian than a successful revolution. But this was a very hard lesson for anarchists to take on board.

Does all of the above mean that the Trotskyists had no contacts with Rebull or with the Friends of Durruti? No.

In any case the POUM left (Rebull) and the Friends of Durruti (Balius) had a meeting during the May events, but the numerical slightness of both organizations and the refusal by the Friends of Durruti to issue a joint manifesto with Cell 72 ensured that these contacts failed to produce anything practical.[17]

After the May events, the Group was disowned by the CNT leadership, and although its members were in the end not expelled from the CNT, insofar as the Friends of Durruti always retained a measure of support in the unions' assemblies, they were denied the use of the CNT presses. It was on account of this that the Friends of Durruti Group turned to Rebull, the administrative director of *La Batalla* and Ediciones Marxistas. Rebull, without even bothering to consult the POUM leadership, and honoring the most elementary — though no less risky — duty of solidarity, granted the Group access to the POUM's presses so that they could print the Manifesto which the Friends of Durruti distributed in Barcelona on May 8. [18]

Might this perhaps mean that Rebull had an influence over the Friends of Durruti? **Absolutely not**. Did Moulin's involvement in the Group's interminable discussions mean that Trotskyists had influence with the Group? **Again no**.

There is no denying that there was ongoing contact between militants of the Bolshevik-Leninist Section of Spain and the Friends of Durruti and that several militants of the Group were recipients of the clandestine press produced by the Trotskyists.[19]

However these contacts were not confined to a simple swapping of the underground press produced by each group. The various organizations outlawed in June 1937 kept in touch and shared assets and intelligence in order to stand up to the repression and carry on the fight from their common clandestine circumstances or simply showed solidarity with fellow revolutionaries. Such as in the ongoing campaign calling for solidarity with those indicted in the show trial against the POUM. Or else the intelligence that Captain Narwitsch was a police spy — intelligence passed on to the Trotskyists by militants from the POUM. There was also the underground publication by the same printer Baldomero Palau of issue No. 3 of *La Voz Leninista* and several issues of *El Amigo del Pueblo* on presses located in the Calle Salmerón.[20]

Although the Trotskyists and the Durruti-ists were not in touch prior to May 1937: and although they mounted no joint action despite the contacts that were established during the May events and in the ensuing weeks:

from June onwards after the proscription of the POUM, the Bolshevik-Leninist Section and the Friends of Durruti's newspaper there was a period of solidarity and cooperation between the various underground organizations and indeed of personal friendships between their militants.[21]

So we may conclude that although various groups were in touch with the Friends of Durruti we cannot strictly speak of any significant decisive outside influence upon the Friends of Durruti: **Contacts? yes,** but **influence? no.**

We have already dealt at length with the existence of contacts between Trotskyists, POUMists, Group members and anarchist militants. Contacts that consisted not just of discussion and political debate, exchange and distribution of newspapers but which also culminated in memorable high-risk acts of solidarity in the face of counterrevolutionary and Stalinist repression. A solidarity that was closer to the camaraderie[22] among activists than the ideological or organizational type of proselytizing influence imagined by historians. Or to put it in such a way that it may be comprehensible even to the most fatuous, pompous, lying, conceited sanctimonious hypocrite from the closed and illustrious guild of academic historians — help was tendered to a comrade from a different organization simply because he had shown that he "had balls" and not because of any abstract indeterminate degree of ideological influence in play.

However, there may be those who cannot grasp the meaning of the word solidarity between revolutionaries.

Notes to Chapter 10

1. There were two rival Trotskyist groups in existence in Spain during the civil war: the Bolshevik-Leninist Section led by Munis and the "Le Soviet" group led by "Fosco." We make no references here to "Le Soviet" because it had no dealings with the Friends of Durruti. For this reason we use the term Trotskyist as a synonym for militants of the Bolshevik-Leninist Section.
2. For the "Communist Union Manifesto" as an historiographical error see: Agustin Guillamón "El Manifiesto de Unión Commuistda: un repetido error en la historiografia sobre la guerra civil" in *La História i el Joves historiadors catalans*, Pónencies i Comunicacions de les Primeres Jornades de Joves Historiadors Calalans, celeblades els dies 4, 5 i 6 d'octubre de 1984 (Ediciòns La Magrana Barcelona 1986) and Paul Sharkey *The Friends of Durruti. A Chronology* (Editorial Crisol, Tokyo May 1984)
3. On this point we are in agreement with Paul Sharkey.
4. See Munis's article in No. 2 of *La Voz Leninista* (August 23, 1937) entitled "La Junta revolucionaria y los 'Amigos de Durruti'," wherein Munis analyses

the concept of revolutionary junta championed by the Group in No. 6 of *El Amigo del Pueblo* (August 12, 1937).

5. In his letter to Bolloten written from Cuernavaca and dated June 20, 1946 Balius stated:

> The alleged influence of the POUM or the Trotskyists upon us is untrue. You will appreciate that the Group of us CNT comrades who headed the Group knew perfectly well what we wanted. We were not newcomers to the revolutionary lists. Consequently, all of the claims that have been tossed around are utterly unfounded.
>
> By my reckoning what I have said should be enough. You may describe the Friends of Durruti Group as an attempt by a group of CNT militants to rescue it from the morass in which it found itself and at the same time to salvage the Spanish revolution which had been menaced from the outset by counterrevolutionary forces which the CNT in its ***naiveté*** had failed to eliminate. Especially in Catalonia, where no one could have challenged our supremacy.

In a letter from Hyéres (France) to Paul Sharkey, on September 7, 1974, Balius himself stressed the independence of the Group, confirming the complete absence of contacts between the Friends of Durruti and the Trotskyists and the POUM, ***prior to May 1937***: "We had no contact with the POUM, nor with the Trotskyists, but there was some mixing on the streets, with rifles in hand."

6. Jaime Balius "Por los fueros de la verdad" in *Le Combat syndicaliste* of September 2, 1971.

7. *La Voz Leninista* No. 2, Barcelona, August 23, 1937.

8. In Barcelona the POUM's left was represented by Cell 72, and more specifically by its secretary Josep Rebull, the administrator of *La Batalla* and the Editorial Marxista. Josep Rebull had drafted a counter-proposition in anticipation of the convening of the POUM's second congress, at which he delivered a radical critique of the political policy pursued by the POUM Executive Committee.

9. Reprinted with the permission of The Houghton Library (Harvard University).

10. Reprinted with the permission of The Houghton Library (Harvard University).

11. The leaflet from the Bolshevik-Leninist Section distributed on May 4, 1937 (reconstituted from the facsimile published in *Lutte ouvriere* No. 48, of June 10, 1937) reads:

> Long live the revolutionary offensive! No compromises. Disarm the GNR [Republican National Guard] and the reactionary Assault Guards. This is a crucial juncture. It will be too late next time. Gen-

eral Strike in every industry not working for the war effort until such time as the reactionary government steps down. Proletarian power alone can guarantee military victory. Complete arming of the working class. Long live the CNT-FAI-POUM unity of action! Long live the Revolutionary Front of the Proletariat. Revolutionary Defense Committees in the workshops, factories, barricades, etc. . . ."

12. Munis offered a very lively criticism of the ambiguity and indecision of the so-called POUM left in Barcelona, in the form of Cell 72, which, at the beginning of 1938, would dwindle to its secretary Josep Rebull and no one else: see Grandizo Munis "Carta a un obrero poumista. Ia Bandera de la IV Internaciónal es la única bandera de la revolución proletaria" in *La Voz Leninista* No. 3, of February 5, 1938.

13. In *La Voz Leninista* No. 2 (23 August 1937), Munis made a critique of the notion of the "revolutionary junta" set out in No. 6 of *El Amigo del Pueblo* (August 12, 1937). In Munis's view, the Friends of Durruti suffered from a progressive theoretical decline and a practical inability to influence the CNT, which led them to abandon some positions which the May experience had enabled them to occupy. Munis noted that in May 1937 the Friends of Durruti had issued the call for a "revolutionary junta" alongside "all power to the proletariat": whereas in No. 6 of *El Amigo del Pueblo* (August 12, 1937) the slogan "revolutionary junta" was invoked as an alternative to the "failure of all Statist forms." According to Munis, this represented a theoretical retreat from the Friends of Durruti's assimilation of the May experiences, taking them further away from the marxist notion of the dictatorship of the proletariat, and drawing them back into the ambiguities of the anarchist theory of the State.

14. Reproduced in Pierre Broué *Léon Trotsky. La revolución española (1930-1940)* Vol. II, pp. 405409.

15. José Peirats *El movimiento libertarion en España (1) José Peirats* Colección de Histórid Oral, Fundación Salvador Segui, Madrid, undated.

16. José Peirats *La CNT en la revolución española* three volumes. (Ruedo Ibérico, Paris, 1971). In this, the official history of the CNT, Peirats hardly mentions the Friends of Durruti.

17. Unpublished interview given to Agustin Guillamón by Josep Rebull, as cited previously.

18. Jordi Arquer *História de la fundació. . .* op. cit.

19. In the affidavit taken from Manuel Fernandez ("Munis") by a magistrate and used as part of the book of evidence in the Espionage and High Treason Tribunal of Catalonia versus the militants of the Bolshevik-Leninist Section of Spain, we read: "Questioned as to which anarchist groups the Bolshevik-Leninist Section, of which the deponent ["Munis"] was the general secretary,

was in cahoots with, he states: That they were in cahoots with no one, since, had he been, it would have been with persons who had stopped being anarchists in order to join the Bolshevik-Leninist Section, adding that they used to send the clandestine press they published to some persons who belonged to the 'Friends of Durruti', as well as to UGT and CNT personnel too."

20. As is recorded in the report of the search of Baldomero Palau's printworks, a report taken by the magistrate drafting the indictment against the Trotskyist militants: "In Barcelona, at 8.30 A.M. on the fourteenth of February nineteen hundred and thirty eight, officers [. . .] acting on instructions from above, and carrying a search warrant [. . .] arrived at No. 241, Calle Salmerón, a printworks, in order to effect a scrupulous search, in that it appeared that it was being used for the printing of clandestine publications, in some of which the lawfully constituted government was being attacked.

Once there and in the presence of the Manager of the presses, namely ***Baldomero Palau Millan***, who lives on the premises in the Calle de Cera [. . .] they proceeded to carry out the order, the upshot being that three printer's "mastheads" were found: these, when copies were taken from them turned out as follows: one was the mast-head from *El Amigo del Pueblo*, having in the right hand margin, boxed, writing which stated 'The Public Entertainments clash, which has been resolved happily, was a provocation by Comorera. While our comrades fight at the front, this wretch is busily torpedoing the rearguard. The unity of these workers has frustrated his designs" [text taken from No. 12 of *El Amigo del Pueblo* of February 1, 1938]: another, from *La Voz Leninista* and a third from *El Amigo del Pueblo*: all of which were seized by the duty officers for transmission to their Superiors."

21. See G, Munis's letter of October 2, 1948 from Paris:

> During the May events, the B-L Section contacted the Friends of Durruti, but nothing was coordinated, for practical reasons and also — I imagine although I cannot be certain — because the Friends of Durruti thought they might lose popularity in the CNT if the leadership of the latter were to accuse them of allying themselves with marxists. After the May events there was more friendliness and interaction between the two groups. The influence of both inside the CNT grew considerably. Generally speaking, it was members of the latter who were most involved in distributing *El Amigo del Pueblo* and *La Voz Leninista*."

Munis and Balius, who had never met before May 1937, subsequently struck up a comradely relationship, based on mutual appreciation and respect, ideologically and personally. This friendship flourished in exile in Mexico, since Balius lived in Munis's home for a time, according to Arquer.

11. Conclusions and Concluding Note

The Friends of Durruti Group was an affinity group, like many another existing in anarcho-syndicalist quarters. It was not influenced to any extent by the Trotskyists, nor by the POUM. Its ideology and watchwords were quintessentially in the CNT idiom: it cannot be said that they displayed a marxist ideology at any time. In any event, they displayed great interest in the example of Marat during the French Revolution, and it may be feasible to speak of their having been powerfully attracted by the assemblyist movement of the Parisian sections, by the sans-culottes, the Enrages and the revolutionary government of Robespierre and Saint-Just.

Their objective was nothing less than to tackle the CNT's contradictions, afford it an ideological coherence and wrest it from the control of its personalities and responsible committees in order to return it to its class struggle roots. The Group had been set up to criticize and oppose the CNT's policy of concession after concession,[1] and of course the **collaboration** of anarcho-syndicalists in the central and Generalidad governments. They were against the abandonment of revolutionary objectives and of anarchism's fundamental and quintessential ideological principles, which the CNT-FAI leaders had thrown over in favor of antifascist unity and the need to adapt to circumstances. Without revolutionary theory there is no revolution. If principles were good for nothing other than to be discarded at the first hurdle erected by reality, it might be better to acknowledge that we have no principles. The top leaders of Spanish anarcho-syndicalism imagined themselves skillful negotiators, but they were manipulated like so many puppets.[2] They forswore everything and in return got . . . nothing. These were opportunists without opportunity. The uprising of July 19 had no revolutionary party capable of taking power and making revolution. The CNT had never considered what was to be done once the army mutineers had been defeated. The July victory plunged the anarcho-syndicalist leaders into bewilderment and confusion. They had been overtaken by the masses' revolutionary dynamism. And, not knowing what to do next, they agreed to Companys's suggestion that they set up a Popular Front government in conjunction with the other parties. And they posited a phony dilemma between **anarchist dictatorship** or **antifascist unity and collaboration with the State** for the purposes of winning the war. They had no idea what to do with power, when the failure to take it resulted in its falling into the bourgeoisie's hands. The Spanish revolution was the tomb of anarchism as a revolutionary theory of the proletariat. Such was the origin and motivation behind the Friends of Durruti Group.

However, the Group's boundaries were very plain and well-defined. As were its limitations, too. At no time did they contemplate a break with the CNT. Only utter ignorance of the organizational mechanics of the CNT could lead us to imagine that it was possible to carry out critical or schismatic activity that would not lead to expulsion. In the case of the Friends of Durruti, expulsion was averted thanks to the sympathies they enjoyed among the CNT rank and file membership, albeit at the cost of severe ostracism and near absolute isolation.

The ultimate aim of the Group was to criticize the CNT leaders and to end the policy of CNT participation in government. They sought not only to preserve the "gains" of July but to prosecute and pursue the process of revolution. But their means and their organization were still extremely limited. They were barricade-fighters, not good organizers and indeed were worse theorists, although they did have some good journalists. In May they trusted entirely to the masses' spontaneity. They failed to counter official CNT propaganda. They neither used nor organized militants who were members of the Control Patrols. They issued no instructions to Máximo Franco, a Friends of Durruti member, a delegate of the CNT's Rojinegra Division, which attempted to "go down to Barcelona" on May 4, 1937, only to return to the front (as did the POUM column led by Rovira) following overtures made to it by Molina.[3] The high point of their activities was the poster distributed in late April 1937, in which the overthrow of the Generalidad government and its replacement by a Revolutionary Junta was urged: control of several barricades in the Ramblas during the May events: the reading of a call, addressed to all Europe's workers,[4] for solidarity with the Spanish revolution: distribution around the barricades of the famous May 5th handbill: and the assessment of the May days in the manifesto of May 8th. But they were unable to put these slogans into practice. They suggested the formation of a column to go out and head off troops coming from Valencia: but they soon abandoned the idea in view of the cool reception received by the proposal. After the May events they began publication of *El Amigo del Pueblo*, although they had been disowned by the CNT and the FAI. In June 1937, although they had not been outlawed as the POUM had, they suffered the political persecution that hit the rest of the CNT's membership. Their mouthpiece *El Amigo del Pueblo* was published clandestinely from issue No. 2 (May 26) onwards, and its managing editor Jaime Balius endured a series of jail terms. Other Friends of Durruti members lost their posts or their influence, like Bruno Lladó, a councilor on Sabadell city council. Most of the Durruti-ists had to endure FAI-sponsored attempts[5] to have them expelled from the CNT. In spite of all of which they carried on issuing their newspaper clandestinely and in mid1938 they issued the pamphlet *Hacia una nueva revolución*, by which time the counterrevolution's success had proved final and overwhelming and the republicans had already lost the war.

Their chief tactical proposals were summed up in the following slogans: trade union management of the economy, federation of municipalities, militia-based army, revolutionary program, replacement of the Generalidad by a Revolutionary Junta, concerted CNT-FAI-POUM action.

If we had to sum up the historical and political significance of the Friends of Durruti, we should say that it was the failed attempt, originating from within the bosom of the libertarian movement, to establish a revolutionary vanguard that would put paid to the CNT-FAI's collaborationism and defend and develop the revolutionary "gains" of July.

The attempt was a failure because they showed themselves incapable, not just of putting their slogans into practice, but even of effectively disseminating their ideas and offering practical guide-lines for campaigning on behalf of them. The Group was constituted as an FAI affinity group. Perhaps the terror-stricken bourgeoisie and the disguised priest regarded them as savage beasts, but their numbers included journalists like Balius and Callejas, militia column commanders like Pablo Ruiz, Francisco Pellicer and Máximo Franco and councilors like Bruno Lladó. For their distant origins we have to go back to the libertarians who shared the revolutionary experience of the Upper Llobregat insurrection in January 1932 and to the FAI's "Renacer" affinity group between 1934 and 1936. Their more immediate roots lay in the opposition to militarization of the militias (especially in the Gelsa sector and within the Iron Column) and in the defense of revolutionary gains and criticism of the CNT's collaborationism as set out in articles published in *Solidaridad Obrera* (between July and early October 1936), in *Ideas* and *La Noche* (between January and May 1937), by Balius in particular. Their campaign weapons were the handbill, the poster, the newspaper and the barricade: but a split or rupture was never contemplated as a weapon, any more than exposure of the CNT's counterrevolutionary role, or, during the May events at any rate, confronting the CNT leaders in an effort to counter the CNT-FAI's defeatist counsels.

Yet the historical significance of the Friends of Durruti cannot be denied. And it resides precisely in their status as an internal opposition to the libertarian movement's collaborationist policy. The political importance of their emergence was immediately detected by Nin, who devoted an approving, hopeful article to them,[6] on the grounds that they held out the prospect of the CNT masses' espousing a revolutionary line and opposing the CNT's policy of appeasement and collaboration.

Hence the interest which the POUM and Trotskyists[7] displayed in bringing the Friends of Durruti under their influence — something in which they never succeeded.

The main theoretical contributions of the Group to anarchist thinking can be summed up as these:

1. The need for a revolutionary program.
2. Replacement of the capitalist State by a Revolutionary Junta, which must stand by to defend the revolution from the inevitable attacks of counterrevolutionaries.

Anarchists' traditional apoliticism meant that the CNT lacked a theory of revolution. In the absence of a theory, there is no revolution, and the failure to assume power meant that it was left in the hands of the capitalist State. In the estimation of the Friends of Durruti Group, the CAMC (Central Antifascist Militias Committee) was a class collaborationist agency, and served no purpose other than to prop up and reinforce the bourgeois State which it neither could nor wished to destroy. Hence the Friends' advocacy of the need to set up a Revolutionary Junta, capable of coordinating, centralizing and reinforcing the power of the countless workers', local, defense, factory, militians' etc. committees, which alone held power between July 19 and September 26. This power was diffused through numerous committees, which held all power locally, but by failing to federate, centralize and reinforce one another, were channeled, whittled down and converted by the CAMC into Popular Front councils, into the management boards of unionized firms and the battalions of the Republican army. Without utter destruction of the capitalist State, the revolutionary events of

July 1936 could not have opened the way to a new structure of workers' power. The decline and ultimate demise of the revolutionary process was inevitable. However, the tension between the CNT-FAI's reformist anarchism and the Friends of Durruti's revolutionary anarchism was not plain and stark enough to provoke a split which would have clarified the contrasting stances of them both.

So, although the political thinking set out by the Friends of Durruti was an attempt to accommodate the reality of the war and revolution in Spain within anarcho-syndicalist ideology, one of the primary grounds on which it was rejected by the CNT membership was its authoritarian, "marxist" or "Bolshevistic" flavor. From which we may conclude that the Friends of Durruti were trapped in a *cul de sac*. They could not embrace the collaborationism of the CNT's leadership cadres and the progress of the counterrevolution: but when they theorized about the experiences of the Spanish revolution, that is, concluded that there was a need for a Revolutionary Junta to overthrow the bourgeois republican government of the Generalidad of Catalonia and use force to repress the agents of the counterrevolution, they were dubbed marxists and authoritarians,[8] and thereby lost any chance they might have had of making recruits from among the CNT rank and file. We have to wonder if the Friends of Durruti's dilemma was not merely a reflection of Spanish anarcho-syndicalism's theoretical inability to face up to the problems posed by the war and the revolution.

We cannot wind up this study without a concluding note expressing our political repugnance and our repudiation, in our capacity as readers of history, of those who, hiding behind their alleged academic objectivity,[9] dare to defame, judge, condemn, insult and hold up to ridicule persons and organizations from the workers' movement — all from a **bourgeois** standpoint, which they of course consider to be scientific and impartial, although they may have utilized no methodology other than misrepresentation of the facts and the most asinine nonsense.

There may be those who take the line that the criticisms articulated here of the Friends of Durruti's and the CNT's political stances have, on occasion, been very harsh: we shall be satisfied if they are also regarded as rigorous and class-based, and our response will be that the repression that the defeat of the proletariat brought in its wake was **even harsher**.

Balius was not the crippled, bloodthirsty ogre as which the terror of the bourgeois and the cleric depicted him in 1937: or as he is represented today by the "comic books" from the Catalanist publishing house of the Benedictines of Montserrat, and/or the unwarranted hogwash from quite a few academic historians. Balius was a modest, intelligent, honest person, a

coherent and intransigent and extremely commonsensical revolutionary. But even if Balius had been — as he was not — the demon as which the terrified clergy and bourgeoisie imagined him, that would not have altered our assessment of the Friends of Durruti one iota. Precisely because we have acknowledged, analyzed and repeatedly emphasized in this work the limitations of the band of revolutionaries known as the **Friends of Durruti Group**, we cannot close without paying tribute to the memory of a working class organization which embodied **the proletariat's class consciousness** and which strove, at a given point, and with a full complement of limitations and shortcomings, to fill the role of a revolutionary vanguard.

In Barcelona it was and still is possible to overhear expressions of hatred and contempt relating to Durruti and "his friends" coming from the lips of the class enemy: however, in working class circles, the mythic Durruti, the huge proletarian demonstration at his funeral, the indomitable rebelliousness of the Durruti-ists, and the revolutionary anarchist feats of July 19 have always been spoken of with respect. During the long night of Francoism, anonymous hands scrawled the names on the unmarked graves of Durruti and Ascaso. It is not the task of the historian to respect myth: but it is the task of the historian to confront defamation, misrepresentation and insult when they pass themselves off as historical narrative.

And although we tackle that thankless task, we prefer to draw the lessons that matter to the class struggle. It should be enough to bear two pictures in mind. In the first, we see a humble, persuasive, loquacious Companys on July 21 , offering to make room for anarchist leaders in an Antifascist Front government, on the grounds that they had routed the military fascists and power was in the streets. In the second, we see a brazen, cornered Companys beseeching the Republican government on May 4 to order the air force to bomb the CNT's premises. The film of the revolution and the war is running between these two pictures.

May 1937 was incubated in July 1936. The Friends of Durruti Group had realized that revolutions are totalitarian or are defeated: therein lies its great merit.

Notes to Chapter 11

1. According to Arquer [letter to Bolloten dated 16 July 1971, deposited with the Hoover Institution] the Friends of Durruti were a passing eruption which at one point articulated the deepest feelings of the CNT membership in Catalonia, and, had the anarchists succeeded that tendency might well have consolidated itself and grown, but once defeated, they lost all influence and their leaders came within an ace of expulsion.

2. The degree of familiarity and day to day friendly relations between Federica Montseny and the Russian ambassador, Rosenberg, defies belief, and the assistance and fillip which Abad de Santillán attempted to afford a discredited Companys likewise defies imagination. The sublime saintliness of the anarchist leaders accounts for the ease with which they were manipulated.
By way of an example of what we are saying, see Frederica Montseny's own declarations (in Agusti Pons *Converses amb Frederica Montseny: Frederica Montseny, sindicalisme i acràcia* [Laia, Barcelona, 1977, pp. 169-170]):

> Before setting off for Russia, having been recalled, Ambassador Rosenberg who had become my friend — called to see me [. . .] [I] was staying at the Metropol, which was the seat of the Russian embassy. I was to be one of the last government figures to arrive in Valencia, when the government, in view of the military situation, resolved to move there from Madrid. Neither the Ministry of Health nor myself, who held that portfolio, could find anywhere to settle in. Everywhere was occupied. Until, eventually, the Russians very kindly turned over to me one of the floors of the hotel which had been turned into their embassy. Many a time I found a bouquet of red carnations in my room. But the flowers were only an excuse for rummaging around the whole room.

But the following excerpt from Frederica Montseny's letter, dated Toulouse May 31, 1950, to Burnett Bolloten, strikes us as even more revealing:

> Rosenberg very kindly offered me two rooms in the Hotel Metropol [in December 1936, in Valencia] which was occupied by the Soviet Embassy and its personnel. I reckon that his intention must have been to keep me continually under his influence. I accepted, after consultation with Vazquez, who had just been appointed secretary of our National Committee, and I moved into the Metropol. I ate in the Hotel dining room, mingling with the Russian officials, and, very often, in the Ambassador's personal quarters. Virtually every night, he would invite me in for coffee. There I met Marty, Gallo, Kleber, Blucher, Tito [?] and Gorev, whom I had met before in Madrid. And very often I saw, or my secretary who was nosier or less discreet than me, saw Alvarez del Vayo, Garcia Oliver and López coming and going from Rosenberg's quarters. Occasionally, Mariano R. Vázquez was invited along with me, passing many a long hour in lazy conversation, drinking cup after cup of coffee or tea.

See also the testimony of Abad de Santillán, from the FAI's Peninsular Committee: "We were none too pleased with the power for which the Militias Committee stood and could impose. There was a government, there was the Generalidad and we would have liked the thousands of problems and gripes and demands brought to us every day to have been heard and resolved by the lawful government, which was not recognized by the broad masses. During some casual get together, we invited President Companys to attend so that people might get used to regarding him as a friend of ours, whom they could trust." [Diego Abad de Santillán *Alfonso XIII, la II Republica, Francisco Franco* (Juúcar, Madrid, 1979, p. 349)]

3. Letter from Balius to Burnett Bolloten, dated Cuernavaca July 13, 1946.

4. According to Pablo Ruiz's claims in "Elogio póstumo de Jaime Balius," in *Le Combat syndicaliste/Solidaridad Obrera* of January 9, 1981.

5. See the articles in which the FAI moved that the Friends of Durruti be expelled, in *Boletin de información y orientación orgánica del Comite peninsular de la Federación Anarquista Iberica*, like "La desautorización de la entidad 'Amigos de Durruti"' in No. 1, Barcelona, May 20, 1937, and "La sanción publica a los inteurantes dc la agrupación Los Amigos de Durruti" in No. 3, June 6, 1937.

6. Andres Nin "Ante el peligro contrarrevoluciónario ha llegado la hora de actuar" in *La Batalla* of March 4, 1937.

7. See Munis's article on the Friends of Durruti in *La Voz Leninista* No. 2, August 23, 1937, entitled "La junta revoluciónaria y los 'Amigos de Durruti.'"

8. The description 'authoritarian,' a term of abuse among libertarians, was not, however, a product of CNT propaganda, since one of the most significant of the Group's theoretical advances was its assertion of the authoritarian, or totalitarian character of any revolution. This is an assertion which the Friends of Durruti reiterated on several occasions. It was first made in an article which Balius published on December 6, 1936, under the title "El testamento de Durruti," and was placed in Durruti's mouth in the course of his harangue from the Madrid front on November 5, 1936: and the last mention was in the 1978 introduction to the English language edition of the pamphlet *Towards a Fresh Revolution*, which reads thus:

> In that booklet back in 1938, we said that all revolutions are totalitarian.

9. Spanish historiography on the civil war has turned from being ***militant history*** written by protagonists and eyewitnesses of the civil war, with all of the dangers implicit in that, but also the irreplaceable passion of someone who does not gamble with words because previously he gambled with his very life, into ***inane academic history*** written by ninnies and characterized by nonsense, incomprehension and indeed contempt for the militants and organizations of the workers' movement. Still, there are a few honorable exceptions — among them the lines of inquiry opened up by Vilanova, Monjo and Vega, which we might describe as an ***academic history*** that fulfills its function, and requires the addition of no further qualifying term.

Kate Sharpley Library

Comrades and Friends —

No doubt some of you will be aware of the work of the **Kate Sharpley Library and Documentation Centre**, which has been in existence for the last eight years. In 1991 the Library was moved from a storage location in London to Northamptonshire, where we are now in the process of creating a database of the entire collection. At the same time, a working group has been formed to over see the organisation and running of the Library. The catalogue of the Library material will be published by AK Press (Edinburgh).

The Library is made up of private donations from comrades, deceased and living. It comprises several thousand pamphlets, books, newspapers, journals, posters, flyers, unpublished manuscripts, monographs, essay, etc., in over 20 languages, covering the history of our movement over the last century. It contains detailed reports from the IWA (AIT/IAA), the Anarchist Federation of Britain (1945-50), the Syndicalist Workers Federation (1950-1979) and records from the anarchist publishing houses, Cienfuegos Press, ASP and others. Newspapers include near complete sets of Black Flag, Freedom, Spain and the World, Direct Actions (from 1945 onwards), along with countless others dating back 100 years. The Library also has a sizeable collection of libertarian socialist and council communist materials which we are keen to extend.

The Kate Sharpley Library is probably the largest collection of anarchist material in England, and, in order to extend and enhance the collection, we ask all anarchist groups and publications worldwide to add our name to their mailing list. We also appeal to all comrades and friends to *donate* suitable material to the Library. *All* donations are welcome and can be collected. The Katė Sharpley Library (KSL) was named in honour of Kate Sharpley, a First World War anarchist and anti-war activist — one of the countless "unknown" members of our movement so ignored by "official historians" of anarchism. The Library regularly publishes lost areas of anarchist history.

Please contact us if you would like to use our facilities. To receive details of our publications, send a stamped addressed envelope to:

KSL, BM Hurricane, London WC1N 3XX, England

Friends of AK Press

In the last 12 months, AK Press has published around 15 new titles. In the next 12 months we should be able to publish roughly the same, including new work by Murray Bookchin, CRASS, Daniel Guerin, Noam Chomsky, Jello Biafra, new audio work from Noam Chomsky, plus more. However, not only are we financially constrained as to what (and how much) we can publish, we already have a huge backlog of excellent material we would like to publish sooner, rather than later. If we had the money, we could easily publish 30 titles in the coming 12 months.

Friends of AK Press is a way in which you can directly help us try to realize many more such projects, much faster. Friends pay a minimum of $15/£10 per month into our AK Press account. All moneys received go directly into our publishing. In return, Friends receive (for the duration of their membership), automatically, as and when they appear, one copy free of every new AK Press title. Secondly, they are also entitled to 10 percent discount on everything featured in the current AK Distribution mail-order catalog (upwards of 3,000 titles), on any and every order. **Friends**, if they wish, can be acknowledged as a **Friend** in all new AK Press titles.

To find out more on how to contribute to Friends of AK Press, and for a Friends order form, please do write to:

AK Press
PO Box 40682
San Francisco, CA
94140-0682

AK Press
P.O. Box 12766
Edinburgh, Scotland
EH8 9YE

CPSIA information can be obtained
at www.ICGtesting.com
Printed in the USA
LVHW010417081021
699885LV00003B/38

9 781873 176542